Mary,
Mother and Disciple

Mary,
Mother and Disciple

*From the Scriptures
to the Council of Ephesus*

Joseph A. Grassi

---

with
A Woman's Response and Poems
by
Carolyn Grassi

Michael Glazier, Inc.
Wilmington, DE

About the author

Joseph A. Grassi is a professor in the Department of Religious Studies at Santa Clara University. He studied Theology and Scripture at Rome, where he earned his S.S.L. degree at the Pontifical Biblical Institute. His principal area of research is the New Testament and Christian Origins. Among his previous books are *God Makes Me Laugh: A New Approach to Luke, The Secret of Paul the Apostle* and *Broken Bread and Broken Bodies: The Lord's Supper and World Hunger*. He has contributed articles to the *Jerome Biblical Commentary* (Ephesians, Colossians) and has written for the *Catholic Biblical Quarterly, Bible Today, New Testament Studies,* and *Novum Testamentum.*

First published in 1988 by Michael Glazier, Inc., 1935 West Fourth Street, Wilmington, Delaware 19805.

Library of Congress Catalog Card Number: 87-82348
International Standard Book Number: 0-89453-640-0

Typography by Angela Meades.
Printed in the United States of America.

To Mary,
in gratitude and love

CONTENTS

INTRODUCTION

The purpose and scope of this book is quite different from that of many other books that have been written about Mary, Mother of Jesus. Many of these might be called "mariological." This means that they try to extract and sometimes even eke out all they can about the person of Mary by examining all the texts that refer to her. This type of approach can have the undesired effect of divorcing Jesus' mother from her proper place within early Christian communities. It may thus result in an unrealistic picture of her, one that either exaggerates her role or diminishes her place in the early Christian church.

We are faced with a great problem in the change that has taken place in Christianity. Any traveler to Europe quickly notices that the great cathedrals, Chartres, Notre Dame and many others bear witness to the centuries of prominence she had in popular Christian devotion. The Protestant Reformation, beginning from the 16th Century, changed all this for a large part of Christianity. With the reformers' emphasis on faith alone, centered in Christ, popular devotion to Mary was looked down upon as an aberration and even at times as idolatry.

In the Roman Catholic Church, almost in reaction to Protestantism, popular devotion to Mary continued to increase. It was to Mary's shrines and cathedrals that people came with their longings and petitions. Stories of Mary's apparitions attracted millions of pilgrims from all over the world to places such as Lourdes and Fatima. They came not only for healing but for help in their daily lives. Novenas and popular devotions to Mary filled Catholic churches. Religious instruction and even official papal teachings kept apace with popular devotion. Hundreds of books were written about Mary. She was described as mediatrix of all graces; her bodily assumption into heaven was defined to be official dogma by the pope.

However, the Vatican Council in the mid-Sixties put a stop to centuries of Marian emphasis in the Catholic Church. The male bishops and cardinals from all over the world deposed the woman who had reigned as queen for so many centuries. They rejected by a narrow majority a separate document on Mary that would have extolled her special place and privileges. Instead she was placed in the document on the church, where she became a model of faith for Christians. The Vatican Council leadership had a profound effect on Marian teachings and devotion. Prominent authors condemned the "aberrations" of the past and the harm (in their opinion) caused by "excessive" devotion to Mary. Many images of Mary were removed from churches. A more Christo-centric liturgy was developed that had little place for Mary. Under careful supervision of the bishops, Catholic education and preaching adopted the teachings of Vatican II on the subordinate role of Mary. All of this had a profound effect on popular devotion to Mary, which has steadily decreased since that time.

Our purpose is to study Mary within the living context of these early communities. What were the needs, problems, difficulties and crises of these churches that led them to portray Jesus' mother in the way they did? To discover this, we must investigate the documents and letters that witness the thought patterns of these groups. Such an investigation will lead us to discover the true place that Mary found within the memory, beliefs, and theology of early Christian communities. Some surprises will result from this study. On the one hand, some sources will indicate that little if any thought was given to Mary's role; others will point to a possible negative attitude; still others will show that Mary had so a prominent place that we will have to reform the attitude that devotion to Jesus' mother in the later church represents an aberration from or exaggeration of views in early Christian communities.

What about the future? Chapter 12 by Carolyn Grassi is a woman's response to Mary in view of the great modern revolution in women's position in society. Her sensitive poetry presents Mary as an enduring female archetype and is a fitting conclusion to the book.

1

Pauline Literature and the Missing Mother of Jesus

By the letters of Paul we mean first of all those that are most certainly from the author himself. These include Romans, 1 and 2 Corinthians, Galatians, Philippians, 1 Thessalonians, and Philemon. These constitute the earliest Christian literature, composed approximately between 49 and 58 A.D. Then there are other letters written in Paul's name but not with the same degree of certainty about their authenticity. These are 2 Thessalonians, Colossians, Ephesians, 1 and 2 Timothy, Titus. In all of these letters there is no direct mention of Mary, the Mother of Jesus. There are, however, indirect references to her, as well as texts that shed light on her place in the early church. It is to these that we now turn our attention.

GALATIANS

In this letter Paul describes a visit he made to Jerusalem not many years after his conversion. He makes special note of the fact that he saw James, the brother of the Lord (1:19). In a later visit, some fourteen years later, James is described as one of the pillars of the church with whom Paul conferred (2:9). In the following chapter, this same James seems to be the respected leader of a group of Jewish Christians who come to Antioch, presumably from Jerusalem (2:11). The expression "Brother of the Lord" in its usual meaning means an actual blood brother, although it is capable of a broader sense.

As a close relative of the earthly Jesus, James had a strong position of authority in the early church. He appears also to have been one of the very early Christian believers. This is brought out by the fact that Paul names him among those privileged by a special apparition of the risen Jesus (1 Cor. 15:7). He seems to be the eldest living son of Mary after Jesus' death, since he is named first as Jesus' brother followed by the names of Joses, Judas and Simon in Mark 6:3.

All of this is important as indirect information about Mary. Her beliefs would hardly have differed from those of James who succeeded to Jesus' prominent position as her first-born son if we rely on the later references in Matthew 1:25 and Luke 2:7. Of course, the much later text of Acts 1:14 names Mary explicitly as being among the first believers assembled at Jerusalem waiting for the coming of the Spirit. However, a more detailed discussion of this text in the context of Luke-Acts will come later.

We can conclude from the important references to James in Galatians that Mary was among early Christian believers. Her role as mother of Jesus would certainly have given her a certain pre-eminence among them. Because early Christians regarded themselves as Jesus' family, they addressed one another as brother and sister, using the title of "mother" or "father" for the older or more respected community members. They did so on the basis of Jesus' words that the new family of disciples were to be called his own brothers, sisters, or mother (Mark 3:35). A later example of how this was put into practice is found in 1 Timothy 5:1 where the author writes "Treat younger men like brothers, older women like mothers, younger women like sisters in all purity." Mary, then, would have a special title of "mother" in the early Christian community, not only as an older respected woman, but as a foremost believer and above all as the mother of Jesus.

A second text from Galatians appears at first glance to have important information about Mary. It reads:

> But when the time had fully come, God sent his Son, born of woman, born under the law, to redeem those who were under the law, so that we might receive adoption as sons. (4:4-5)

We say "at first glance," because without any other context it would seem that the words "his Son" are connected with the following phrase "born of a woman." In other words, the unusual birth of Jesus from a woman would indicate that the child was God's Son. However, the meaning of the words in their context will not allow us to take that meaning. The emphasis on the words "God's Son" is that of obedience.[1] The contrast is being made between the obedience of a son and that of a slave or custodian under the law. In 3:23 Paul has written, "Before faith came, we were confined under the law, kept under restraint until faith should be revealed. So that the law was our custodian until Christ came." In addition, the words *"God sent his Son* have a strong obedience motif. The words "born of a woman" are a biblical expression bringing out the human condition in contrast to God. Thus Job writes, "Man that is born of a woman is of few days and full of trouble" (14:1). While Mary is certainly this woman in the Galatians passage, the text actually tells us nothing about her.

GALATIANS 4:22-31

In these verses Paul makes his famous contrast between those born according to the spirit and those born according to the flesh (28-29). The argument starts off as follows:

---

[1] Carolyn Osiek contrasts between the obedience to slave pedagogues, "baby sitters," and the full mature obedience of a son to a father (pp. 44-47).

> It is written that Abraham had two sons, one by a slave and one by a free woman. But the son of the slave was born according to the flesh, the son of the free woman through promise. Now this is an allegory: these women are two covenants. One is from Mount Sinai, bearing children for slavery; she is Hagar. (4:22-24)

The free woman in the story is Sarah, the wife of Abraham. In verse 26, she is identified with "the Jerusalem above" which is free and which is our mother. Sarah is thus presented as the mother of believers in the promise and of those who are free. The text is similar to that in Romans where Paul writes, "For this is what the promise said, 'About this time I will return and Sarah shall have a son'" (9:9). This picture of Sarah as a model for believers is found elsewhere in the N.T. as well. In Hebrews, we have the text, "By faith Sarah herself received power to conceive, even when she was past the age, since she considered him faithful who had promised" (11:11). Women who imitate Sarah in her obedience are called "her children" in 1 Peter 3:6.

This image of Sarah as a mother and model of believers will be very valuable in Luke's gospel, where it will be shown that the evangelist seems to be presenting a portrait of Mary, mother of believers based on a parallel with Sarah. Along with the consensus of the scholars who wrote *Mary in The New Testament*,[2] we do not think that Paul's reference to one "born according to the Spirit" (Isaac) has anything to do with the virginal conception of Jesus.

ROMANS 1:3-4

This verse and parallels in Paul are of key importance in understanding why there is so little about Mary in Paul and so much in the gospels, especially Matthew, Luke and John.

---

[2]Pp. 45-49. The immediate context of a contrast between the birth of Ishmael "according to the flesh," and Isaac born "according to the promise or spirit" seems to be the key to its meaning.

> ...the gospel concerning his Son, who was descended from David according to the flesh and constituted Son of God in power according to the Spirit of holiness by his resurrection from the dead, Jesus Christ our Lord.

Here we can briefly sum up the exegesis outlined by J. Fitzmyer and a cooperating group of scholars.[3] An important key to the meaning is the contrast in the two halves of the verse:

descended (born)	constituted
from (the seed of) David	Son of God in power
according to the flesh	according to the Spirit
	by his resurrection from the dead

This is all written to describe "Jesus Christ our Lord" at the end of the verse. On the left hand side, we find what may be called prerequisites for being Messiah. These include Jesus' birth as a descendant of David. Here, of course, Mary is essential as Jesus' mother. However, on the right side we find what actually makes Jesus Messiah and Son of God. It is the Spirit at work in Jesus' resurrection that constitutes him as Son of God. The word *Messiah* comes from the Hebrew root meaning "to anoint." The Spirit has anointed and fully immersed Jesus in its power by transforming him and raising him from the dead to make him the messianic Son of God. This connection between Spirit and anointing is found in the Old Testament. For example, Isaiah writes, "The Spirit of the Lord God is upon me because the Lord has anointed me" (61:1).

Not only in this text, but throughout Paul's letters, the Spirit is especially manifest in the resurrection of Jesus. The resurrection body of Jesus as well as of Christians is Spirit-body which Paul calls a *soma pneumatikon* in 1 Cor. 15:44.

---

[3] *Mary in the New Testament*, pp. 34-40.

Thus Jesus becomes Messiah for believers through his Spirit-enabled resurrection from the dead. Only the later written gospels will teach that Jesus was Messiah from the time of his earthly birth. Paul's christological doctrine is centered[4] on the death and resurrection of Jesus.

From the above, we can understand why there is so little about Mary in the letters of Paul. She is indeed the mother of Jesus, but as yet there is no understanding of her as mother of the Messiah, Son of God. This is for the simple reason that Jesus is being preached as Messiah and Son of God to the Pauline communities as a result of his resurrection from the dead, but not as yet from the time of his earthly birth.

Summary: In Galatians, we have seen that the important place of James, brother of Jesus, probably indicates that the family of Jesus, especially his mother Mary, had an important place as being among the early believers in the Christian community. As mother of Jesus, she would have a special title of honor as "mother" that was granted to older and respected women. However, she would not as yet be considered as mother of the messianic Son of God because Pauline preaching connected this with the resurrection of Jesus, not with his earthly birth. Paul, however, paved the way for a later presentation of Mary as mother of all believers by his description of Sarah as model and mother of believers in Galatians 4:22-31.

---

[4]David Stanley's study shows how all Paul's Theology is centered about Jesus' death/resurrection. Cf. also, J. Grassi, *The Secret of Paul the Apostle*.

2

Mark and the Family of Jesus

We will study first the gospel of Mark, but without a presupposition that it is the earliest of the gospels. Mark contains no account of the conception and birth of Jesus as do Matthew and Luke, as well as no mention of Jesus' pre-existence as the Word of God as in the prologue of John. We will see later that in Matthew and Luke, Jesus is Messiah from his birth. However, in Mark, Jesus appears on the scene at the Jordan river for his baptism at the hands of John the Baptist. At this moment the Spirit descends upon him and a voice from heaven designates him as Messiah and Son of God:

> In those days Jesus came from Nazareth of Galilee and was baptized by John in the Jordan. And when he came up out of the water, immediately he saw the heavens opened and the Spirit descending upon him like a dove; and a voice came from heaven "You are my beloved Son; with you I am well pleased." (1:9-11)

The descent of the Spirit is Jesus' anointing as Messiah, and from this point forward he begins his messianic career as the Spirit drives him into the wilderness (1:12). We immediately notice how different this is from the Pauline letters. There, Jesus' messianic anointing by the Spirit takes place only at his resurrection. However, in Mark there is a similarity to Paul in that Jesus' messianic anointing is known only to himself. The vision of the descending spirit-dove and the hearing of the declaration, "You are my beloved son" appear to be perceived only by Jesus, and not by anyone else.

This is part of what is called the Messianic secret in Mark's gospel. It is something that will only be known to others through Jesus' suffering and death. Only at his trial before the Sanhedrin does Jesus acknowledge that he is Son of God to answer the official question of the high priest, "Are you the Christ, the Son of the Blessed?" (14:61). Again, it is only at the foot of the cross that anyone else openly acknowledges him to be son of God. In this case, it is the Roman centurion who states, "Truly this man was the Son of God" when he saw how Jesus had died (15:39). The crowds and even Jesus' disciples consistently do not understand who Jesus really is. Peter does say to Jesus "You are the Christ" (8:29). However, Peter's understanding seems to be incomplete since Jesus tells him to be silent in the next verse, and then rebukes him for not accepting that he must suffer and die (8:31-33).

All this will affect Mark's view of Jesus' mother. Since Mark tells us nothing of Jesus' birth, we would expect that Mary would be included among those who do not understand who Jesus is in this gospel. This will be confirmed as we treat the various episodes where Jesus' mother and family are mentioned.

WHO ARE JESUS' FAMILY? (3:20-35)

> Then he went home; and the crowd came together again, so they could not even eat. And when his family heard it, they went out to seize him, for they said, "He is beside himself." (3:19b-21)

The translation "his family" is for a literal Greek "his own," which by itself would be ambiguous. However, "his family" seems a very probable translation since the section ends with Mary and the family calling Jesus away from a house crowded with disciples, where there seems to be an intended contrast between Jesus' natural family and his new family of disciples (3:31-35). The description of Jesus' family appears to be part of a whole context of opposition and lack of understanding. The next verse describes the scribes who came from Jerusalem and accused him of being possessed by Beelzebul, and by the prince of devils (3:22).

> And his mother and his brethren came; and standing outside they sent to him and called him. And a crowd was sitting about him; and they said to him, "Your mother and your brethren are outside, asking for you." And he replied, "Who are my mother and my brethren?" And looking around on those who sat about him, he said, "Here are my mother and my brethren! Whoever does the will of God is my brother, and sister, and mother." (3:31-35)

This story concludes the episode beginning with the statement that Jesus' family went out to seize him (3:21). There is a definite contrast between Jesus' mother and family outside, and the group that is inside. The mother and brethren are attempting to use their family authority to get Jesus to come out. Jesus, however, takes a very definite stand by turning around to his disciples and publicly stating that they are his new family—mother, brothers, and sisters. It is not that Jesus' family is being singled out for their opposition, but rather they are part of the whole picture of incomprehension[5] in Mark's gospel.

THE BROTHERS AND SISTERS OF JESUS (6:1-6)

> He went away from there and came to his own country; and his disciples followed him. And on the sabbath he

[5]e.g., W.H. Harrington, (pp. XIV-XV).

began to teach in the synagogue; and many who heard him were astonished, saying, "Where did this man get all this? What is the wisdom given to him? What mighty works are wrought by his hands! Is not this the carpenter, the son of Mary and brother of James and Joses and Judas and Simon, and are not his sisters here with us?" And Jesus said to them, "A prophet is not without honor, except in his own country, and among his own kin, and in his own house." And he could do no mighty work there, except that he laid his hands upon a few sick people and healed them. And he marveled because of their unbelief.

THE CARPENTER, THE SON OF MARY

It would be important to know if this expression tells us anything definite about Mary. Does the omission of Joseph perhaps hint about Jesus' miraculous conception while his mother was a virgin? First of all, if this were so, it would seem unlikely for Matthew in 13:55 to call Jesus the son of the carpenter and Luke in 4:22 to name him the son of Joseph despite the fact that both these evangelists definitely write about the virginal conception of Jesus (Matt. 1:18-25; Luke 1:26-35). John also calls him the son of Joseph (6:42). Secondly, these words are on the lips of the crowd which could hardly know about such a secret. Even Joseph in Matthew's gospel does not know about it until an angel makes it known to him (1:25). Thirdly, if Mark knows about it, it would be difficult to reconcile with his inclusion of the incident previously noted (3:20-21) where the family thinks that Jesus is beside himself and tries to seize him. A knowledge of Jesus' extraordinary conception would have prompted Mark to a greater sense of delicacy by either omitting such an easily misunderstood incident or by describing it in a more favorable light. Also, Mark notes in 6:4 Jesus' statement that a prophet is not without honor except in his own country, and among his own kin, and in his own house. It would be difficult to include such a statement about lack of belief in Jesus' own kin and house if

Mark knew the tradition about Jesus' virginal conception. Both Matthew and Luke, who know about this, omit the phrase "among his own kin" (Matt. 13:57; Luke 4:24). The three above reasons make it seem likely that Mark simply did not know of Jesus' miraculous conception by a virgin that we find in Matthew and Luke.

A much more likely explanation is simply that Joseph was dead, and that Jesus could sometimes be called the son of Mary, or the son of Joseph as in the other evangelists. This is supported by Mark 3:31 where it is Jesus' mother and brethren who come to the house to call Jesus out. It would be unusual for a Jewish mother to head such a group. It would be the natural place of the father to exercise such authority. However, it would be understandable if Joseph were no longer alive.

We conclude that the description of Jesus as carpenter, son of Mary in Mark's gospel is no definite indication of Jesus' miraculous and virginal conception in the womb of Mary. It is more likely that it is a simple indication that Joseph was no longer alive.

DID JESUS HAVE NATURAL BROTHERS AND SISTERS?

If we read only Mark's gospel, we would have to assume that Mary was the mother of a rather large family that included Jesus, brothers named James, Joses, Simon, Judas and at least two unamed sisters (6:3). The Greek word for brother *adelphos* has the first meaning, as in English, of a natural blood brother. The word, as in English, is also capable of a wider meaning. In the Sermon on the Mount, a brother can be a fellow Christian as when Jesus says, "If your brother has something against you, go leave your gift there before the altar and go first be reconciled to your brother" (Matt. 5:23-24). In the Greek Old Testament, *adelphos* can also mean a close relative, such as a cousin. For example, Laban is called the brother of Abraham, whereas in reality he is a cousin (Gen. 24:48). However, the

New Testament does have a special Greek word for cousin, *anepsios*, in Colossians 4:10, so we could conclude that the reference to brothers and sisters in Mark has the normal meaning of an actual blood brother or sister, but does not preclude the possibility of a wider relationship such as a cousin.

However, if Mark is writing about natural brothers and sisters of Jesus, how can this be reconciled with Mary's virginity that we find so explicitly mentioned in Matthew 1:18-25 and Luke 1:26-35? First of all, these texts say nothing of a perpetual virginity. The text in Matthew says that Joseph "knew her not until she had borne a son" (1:25), but leaves it an open question as to her virginity after that. She could well have had other children from normal marital relations. The same is true of Luke. Jesus is Mary's first-born son from a miraculous conception (2:7; 1:26-35) but nothing is said about other children who may have followed. The earliest suggestion in Christian literature that these children were not Mary's but Joseph's from a previous marriage is found in the *Protoevangelium of James*, 9:2. This document, to be discussed in a later chapter, originates around the middle of the 2nd century A.D. It was several centuries before it became general Christian teaching that Mary remained always a virgin. It has also been claimed that the names James and Joses may be those of sons of another Mary who is called the mother of James the younger and Joses (15:40), the mother of Joses (15:47) and the mother of James (16:1). However, the results of scholars'[6] investigations have led to no certain conclusions.

However, the very fact that Jesus' brothers are mentioned by name may tell us something important about them. The gospel of Mark has few personal names. The evangelist is not interested in merely recording names from the past. We saw already in chapter one that Paul's mention of one of the brothers, James, had special significance. As a brother of the Lord he had a special authority in the early church, having

[6]These are summarized in *Mary in the New Testament*, pp. 68-72.

received a special apparition of the risen Jesus. This led us to believe that Jesus' mother and the rest of the family were among the first believers in the new Way. Parallel to this, Mark could also be giving their names because of a tradition that they were among early Christian believers.

Yet if Jesus' brothers did become believers, why would they appear in a rather hostile context in Mark? We already remarked that this falls within the theme of the general misunderstanding of Jesus in Mark. However, there may be also another motive at work. Mark's gospel appears especially directed to Gentiles and presents a Jesus at conflict with his fellow countrymen's traditions and expectations. For example, Mark alone presents Jesus as declaring all foods clean, in contrast to Jewish traditions (7:19). In the early church, there were conflicting opinions on the permanent value of the O.T. ritual laws and food regulations. The Acts of the Apostles tells us that some Christians, Pharisee converts, demanded that all gentile converts be circumcised and obliged to keep all the Jewish traditional biblical regulations. James appears to incline in this direction, for he suggests a compromise whereby the gentiles pledge to avoid non-kosher meats and meats sacrificed to idols (15:1-29). Thus James and those following his leadership would represent Christians opposed to Mark's radical view in this matter. This may also account for the seemingly hostile presentation of Jesus' family in his gospel.

To sum up: From Mark's gospel alone, it would seem that Jesus had blood brothers and sisters, although it is possible for the Greek word *adelphos* to refer to a wider range of relationships. In Mark, Jesus' family does not appear in a favorable light. Yet this may be due to the whole context of Mark, where Jesus' messianic identity is a secret whose complete meaning is revealed to none until his death and resurrection. Also it may be due to the fact that Mark's view of the permanence of Jewish law is opposed to that represented by James and Jesus' family. However, the very mention of the names of Jesus' family members probably shows that Mark recognizes them to have been very important people in the early Christian church. There is no direct mention of Mary's virginity in Mark, and seemingly, no indirect reference either. She is presented as mother of Jesus, but not yet as mother of the messianic Son of God. This goes along with Mark's view that Jesus is anointed as Messiah at his baptism, but this is a secret known to no one but Jesus.

3

The Mother and the Child:
Matthew's Vision of Hope

In chapter one, we saw that the Pauline letters presented Jesus as anointed Messiah and Son of God at his resurrection. In chapter two, Mark's gospel described Jesus as the Messiah from the time of his baptism, although this was a secret known only to Jesus. In Matthew's gospel we will see that a further step takes place. Matthew will present Jesus as Messiah and Son of God throughout his gospel even from the time of his birth. Thus the way will be opened for Mary's unique place in the divine plan in her role as mother of the Messiah.

First we should outline how Matthew openly portrays Jesus as Messiah, Son of God. In this gospel, even at Jesus' birth, the wisemen from the East, after seeing the wondrous star, come to Jerusalem and ask, "Where is he who has been born king of the Jews?" (2:2). The Magi then visit the child and offer gifts (2:11). The voice from heaven at Jesus' baptism appears to be a public declaration of Jesus' messiahship with the words, "This is my beloved son" (3:17). This contrasts with Mark, where the heavenly voice seems to be directed to Jesus only with the words "*You* are my beloved son" (1:11). After Jesus walks on water those in the boat exclaim, "Truly you are the son of God" (14:33; compare Mark 6:49). At Caesarea Philippi, Peter openly proclaims Jesus to be the Messiah, Son of the living God

(16:16). By contrast in Mark, Peter states that Jesus is the Messiah, but is immediately enjoined to be silent, because he misunderstands the meaning of this title (8:29-33).

Why was it so important for Matthew to establish Jesus as Messiah right from the time of his birth? To answer this we must understand some of the conflicts and decisions[7] faced by a large part of Matthew's audience. Many, if not most, were Jewish Christians who continued to observe their traditional Jewish observances. At first, they were hardly distinguished from their fellow Jews. The Acts of the Apostles describes Peter, John and early Christians as frequenting the Temple and keeping the traditional Jewish food laws (2:46; 3:1; 10:9-16).

However, as time went on, differences and conflicts began to emerge between Jewish Christians and their fellow Jews. The war with Rome, 66-70 A.D., was one such occasion. Some of the Jewish rebellion leaders posed as Messiahs chosen by God to lead their people to freedom and victory over Rome. This meant that Jewish Christians were faced with a serious conflict. On the one hand, they wished to fight for their country; on the other hand, to do so would be to abandon Jesus, their Messiah of peace and follow their own military messianic leaders. The gospel of Matthew advised them to "flee to the mountains" from Jerusalem (24:16) rather than do so. Many followed this advice and were branded as traitors to their country in the time of its greatest need.

After the Roman war, other developments also took place. The Pharisee party became increasingly strong and gradually extended its very strict interpretation of Judaism over all the people. In doing so, they tended to be less acceptant of diversity within Judaism and to exclude non-conformists. One such group was the Jewish Christians. Toward the end of the first century we find evidence of a synagogue curse pronounced on "heretics" who may well have included the Jewish Christians. References in Matthew's

---

[7]This is the special contribution of John Meier's analysis of Matthew.

gospel to Jewish persecution (10:27; 5:11) may indicate this malediction.

Within Christian Judaism also, difficulties had arisen. With the loss of the Temple and Roman destruction of their religious capital, the central authority of official Judaism was greatly weakened. Jewish Christians wondered where they should turn for leadership, since Christianity had not yet developed a strong institutional structure. In addition, the Christian apostolate among the Jews was becoming less and less successful. Judeo-Christians were gradually becoming small minorities in Christian communities that were predominantly Gentile. As a consequence, they became less at home in these communities, since their traditional Jewish practices and customs were not respected by many Gentile Christians. This was especially true of the laws concerning foods and table fellowship. An example of difficulties of this kind is found in Acts 11:12 where Peter is questioned about having eaten with "uncircumcised men," and in Acts 15:29 where James advises the community not to eat certain foods in order to avoid offense to Jewish Christians. In view of all these difficulties, it would not be a surprise that many Jewish Christians felt tempted to rejoin their Jewish brothers and sisters under the leadership of the Pharisees.

In addition, there was much debate between Jews and Jewish Christians. We find toward the end of Matthew's gospel an example of Jewish polemic. The accusation was made that the resurrection of Jesus was a fictional story composed by his disciples who stole his body from the grave (28:12-15). This would mean, if true, that Jesus' messiahship was also an afterthought, since it was so closely connected to early Christian preaching about the origins of Jesus, since their readings of Scripture (and the divine plan) required a Messiah from Bethlehem rather than from Nazareth. The question is directly found in John 7:41, where some said,

> Is the Christ to come from Galilee? Has not the Scripture said that the Christ is descended from David, and comes from Bethlehem, the village where David was? (7:41-42)

This question is indirectly found in Matthew 2:3-6, where the magi come to Jerusalem and ask where the newly born king is to be found. The chief priests and scribes answer,

> In Bethlehem, in the land of Judah; for so it is written by the prophet: "And you, O Bethlehem, in the land of Judah, are by no means least among the rulers of Judah: for from you shall come a ruler who will govern my people Israel. (2:5-7; Mic. 5:2)

Another question raised must have been that the origins of the Messiah should have a mysterious nature in apparent contrast to Jesus whose mother, family and relatives were well known (Matt. 13:55-57). Once again the question is directly found in John, where some people say, "Yet we know where this man is from; and when the Christ appears, no one will know where he is from" (7:27). The Scriptures behind such a statement may have been texts like Malachi 3:7 which described a sudden appearance of a messenger of the covenant in the Temple. Or perhaps Micah 5:2 which spoke of the birth of a ruler from Bethlehem "whose origin is from of old from ancient days."

Consequently, it was essential for Matthew to strengthen his Jewish Christian audience by establishing that Jesus was Messiah in perfect accordance with a divine plan found in the Scriptures. This would mean that he was born in Bethlehem, yet in such a mysterious manner that it would point to his nature as Messiah and Son of God. The two terms, Messiah and Son of God, are side by side, since the promise made to David about a future king specified the sonship relationship with the words, "I will be his father, and he shall be my son" (2 Sam. 7:14). These words are echoed by Psalm 2:7, "He said to me, 'You are my son, today I have begotten you.'" Any identification of the Messiah must surely have this father-son relationship. The voice from heaven in Mark's gospel identified Jesus as such. Yet this was not sufficient for Matthew's audience which must find this designation at birth to answer Jewish questions. Accordingly, we turn to the genealogy of Jesus as Matthew's prelude to establishing Jesus' place as Messiah Son of God in the divine plan.

THE GENEALOGY OF JESUS

The very first words of the gospel solemnly announce the accomplishment of the divine plan: "The book of the genealogy of Jesus Christ, the son of David, the son of Abraham." This divine plan was to bring into the world a chosen offspring of Abraham who would be a source of blessing to the whole world according to the promise made to him by God: "I will make of you a great nation, and I will bless you and make your name great, so that you will be a blessing" (Gen. 12:1-2). Consequently, every pregnant woman in the line of Abraham was one more sign of the advance of the Creator's loving plan for the world family.

While every human birth was regarded as a divine miracle, this was especially true when there were extraordinary circumstances that made the birth of such a child seem impossible. In the case of Abraham, he was a hundred years old at the time and his wife Sarah, ninety (Gen. 17:17). Abraham laughed at the very idea when God announced it to him (17:17). Sarah also had her laugh when she heard from a stranger (an angel in disguise) that she would bear a child within a year (18:12). The author notes how impossible this was by writing, "It had ceased to be with Sarah after the manner of women" (18:11). Consequently, when the child was born, it was called Isaac, meaning "laughter," for Sarah exclaimed, "God has made laughter for me; every one who hears will laugh over me" (21:6).

The case of Abraham and Sarah became a model for a unique image of faith in the divine plan. This image or sign was that of a pregnant woman, or a woman bearing a future child despite highly unusual circumstances. This image appears when God said to Abraham,

> I will bless her, and moreover I will give you a son by her;
> I will bless her, and she shall be a mother of nations. (Gen.
> 17:16; see also 17:19; 18:10, 14)

The remaining women identified by name in Matthew's genealogy (Tamar, Rahab, Ruth, Uriah's wife and Mary), also bear children in highly   unusual circumstances, thus bearing witness to a special divine plan. Judah became a father through Tamar, his daughter-in-law disguised as a temple prostitute (Gen. 38:11, 13-16). Rahab, a foreigner and "innkeeper" (prostitute?) was a great grandmother of king David (Matt. 1:5). Ruth was another foreigner from the Moabites, traditional hated enemies of the Jews, yet she contributed to the royal blood of David her grandson. David the king received a special promise from God that he would have a son as well as a permanent dynasty (2 Sam. 7:12-25). Yet this son was the product of adultery resulting in murder (2 Sam. 11:1-12:25). The final birth is that of Jesus, the last member of the line of Abraham. No human father at all takes part in Jesus' birth: "And Jacob the father of Joseph, the husband of Mary of whom Jesus was born, who is called Christ" (1:16). This last is the most unusual birth of all, and the greatest sign of God's plan working in history, so Matthew will proceed to describe it in detail (1:18-25).

THE CHILD AND HIS MOTHER

"Now the birth of Jesus (or simply birth of Christ in some Greek manuscripts) took place in this way" (1:18). Matthew begins to explain the unusual birth, mentioning only Mary the mother whom he has described in 1:16. The author may also have intended to respond to slurs[8] on the circumstances of Jesus' birth, just as he later replied to false stories about Jesus' death (28:15). Regarding Jesus' birth, it appears posssible that at the time of Matthew's gospel some Jews argued that Jesus was a child of fornication. The charge is quite definite beginning with second century literature, but we cannot be certain that it goes back to Matthew's time. If

---

[8]For a thorough discussion and background of this, cf. Raymond Brown, *Birth of the Messiah*, p. 534-42.

Joseph died at an early age, this could have led to Jesus being called the Son of Mary (Mark 6:3) and left the way open to question about the father of Jesus.

"When his mother Mary had been betrothed to Joseph, before they came together she was found to be with child of the Holy Spirit" (1:18b). The betrothal described here is not equivalent to a modern engagement, but corresponds to unique ancient semitic marriage customs. In these customs, the first step in marriage was the contract or betrothal. Then after a period of time, the husband took the bride to his home in a wedding procession which was followed by a marriage feast. Only after this the groom began to live together with his wife. In the in-between period, sexual relations were usually forbidden. However, the man and woman were regarded as legitimately married from the time of the actual contract. This is why, in Matthew's story, the angel told Joseph to take (home) Mary his woman (wife) in 1:20 (cf. 1:24). During the intermediate period, Mary had become pregnant and somehow the news was brought to Joseph who knew, of course, that the child was not his and did not yet know the secret (given to Matthew's audience) that the child came from the intervention of the Holy Spirit.

"Her husband Joseph, being a just man and unwilling to put her to shame, resolved to divorce her quietly" (1:19). Here the definite Greek word for husband is used in the best Greek texts, confirming that they were legally husband and wife. Joseph is a just man, first because he simply could not take the child as his own with all the rights of family inheritance. Secondly, he did not wish to expose Mary to the humiliation of a public accusation of adultery, which had very severe penalties, even a possible stoning to death (Num. 22:22 and John 7:53-8:11 in some ancient texts). The quiet divorce would seem to be a written notice of dismissal on Joseph's part in which, as R. Brown has suggested,[9] some other lighter reason might be given.

[9]p. 128.

> But as he considered this, behold an angel of the Lord appeared to him in a dream, saying, "Joseph, son of David, do not fear to take Mary your wife, for that which is conceived in her is of the Holy Spirit. She will bear a son, and you shall call his name Jesus, for he will save his people from their sins." (1:20-21)

The "considering" or pondering of Joseph in this type of crisis fits the description of being a just man both in accomplishing the Law and in regard to Mary. His deliberations accompanied by prayer received an answer in a dream. In the Old Testament, dreams were a frequent means of divine communication (e.g. to Jacob, in Gen. 28:10-16: to Pharaoh, Gen. 41:1-8). The note that Joseph is son of David is important to indicate his part in the divine plan, since genealogies were patrilineal. Joseph's assumption of the child as his own, especially by giving it a name, would be important in establishing the child as a Son of David.

However, the child's origin as Messiah, Son of God will be through the Holy Spirit. The child will be Son of God in a special sense because he has no human father and thus truly fits God's words to David in regard to the future heir, "I will be father to him and he will be a son" (2 Sam. 7:14). The Holy Spirit as the agent will accomplish this in so total a manner that it will be an anointing qualifying him for the title of Messiah, meaning "anointed one." Because the Spirit is the agent, the term "Son of God" will be left open to a deeper meaning in the gospel of Matthew through reflection on scripture. One of these sources will be Psalm 110, where David refers to his son, the Messiah, as Lord (Matt. 22:41-45; Mark 12:35-37). Jesus' words that David spoke by the Holy Spirit may be hinting at this higher meaning.

> All this took place to fulfil what the Lord had spoken by the prophet, "Behold a virgin shall conceive and bear a son, and his name shall be called Emmanuel" (which means, "God is with us"). (1:22-23)

In its original context, this prophecy was meant to be an extraordinary sign from God through Isaiah that the dynasty of David would continue on through a future king even at a time when Jerusalem was under siege by two kings who planned to eliminate the davidic king and his family (7:1-9). As a sign of hope and victory, Isaiah announced his God-given vision of a young woman (Hebrew version) giving birth to a child and naming it Emmanuel (God is with us) because the child's conception and birth would be a sign of God's presence in the people through the preservation of the dynasty.

However, Matthew reads the ancient Scripture with a present meaning. He believes that the Holy Spirit has a hidden secret meaning in the Isaian Scripture which he has been able to discover with God's help. This process of finding such a secret meaning for one's own time or situation was not new with Matthew. In the Old Testament, Daniel meditated on the prophecy of Jeremiah referring to a return from exile after seventy years (9:2; Jer. 25:11-12). After prayer and fasting, the angel Gabriel revealed to him that the prophecy had a secret meaning for his own time centuries later, which could be understood in terms of seventy weeks of years (9:20-27). Likewise, the Dead Sea Jewish sectarians near the time of Jesus read the scripture of Isaiah 40:3, "In the desert prepare the way of the Lord," which spoke of the exiles' return to Jerusalem following its destruction in 587 B.C. However, the Dead Sea community applied the scripture to their own work in the Judean desert preparing for the coming of the Messiah. Later, Mark has the same scripture refer to John the Baptist preaching the future coming of the Lord (1:3).

The text in Matthew's hands or memory was probably the Greek version of the Old Testament which translated the "young woman" in Isaiah 7:14 (Hebrew) as *parthenos*, which usually meant an actual virgin. Matthew found that the "virgin" in this text had a hidden meaning in the divine plan announcing God's great sign of Mary, the virgin mother, giving birth to a child without a human father and thus guaranteeing "God with us" or *Emmanuel* through this child.

> When Joseph rose from sleep, he did as the angel of the Lord commanded him; he took his wife, but knew her not until she had borne a son; and he called his name Jesus. (1:24)

This verse is an added confirmation of Mary's virginal conception by the Holy Spirit. The word "until" leaves her relationship with Joseph after Jesus' birth to be an open qustion. As noted previously, it is quite possible that Mary afterwards had other natural children by Joseph. Only later church doctrine will declare Mary always a virgin. As evident from the story, Mary's virginity has nothing to do with her personal character, but with the identity of her son.

Chapter Two of Matthew follows up the essential picture already drawn. The Magi come to visit the Messiah, the king of the Jews, and worship him. Additional scriptures from Mic. 5:2 are brought in to indicate the child's birth in Bethlehem. The phrase "the child" is found seven times in this chapter, seemingly in reference to the wonderful child in the vision of Isaiah 7:14. Isaiah's combined vision of child and mother seems to completely preoccupy Matthew. When the wisemen entered the house in Bethlehem, they saw "the child with Mary his mother" (2:11). Matthew uses the expression "the child and his mother" four more times in this short chapter.

The expression Emmanuel (God with us) serves as an introduction to Jesus' life in Matthew's gospel. Jesus is the one who will show that God is with his people by his miraculous deeds and the authority of his words. Likewise, the Emmanuel sign seems to conclude his gospel when Jesus bids farewell to his disciples but gives them an assurance of his continued presence with the words, "*I am with you* always, to the close of the age" (28:20). So it would appear that the sign of Emmanuel continues on in the community of believers.

MARY MOTHER OF THE MESSIAH
IN THE REMAINDER OF MATTHEW

We would expect Matthew's sublime portrait of Mary in the birth accounts to influence his view of her in Jesus' public life. We recall that Mark's account hints at a rather hostile attitude of Jesus' family: they were worried about Jesus being beside himself and went out to seize him (3:21). These verses are not found in Matthew. In addition, Matthew has separated the account from the hostile Beelzebub charges found in Mark 3:22. His view of Mary as mother of the Messiah from birth prompts him to omit or relocate stories that could lead to a misunderstanding of her. Matthew does preserve the last part of the story, but modifies it and presents it as an independent story that could be understood in a very positive manner parallel to the birth accounts. We can observe this much better if we place the two stories in Mark and Matthew in parallel columns.

Mark 3:31-35	*Matthew* 13:6-50
And his mother and his brothers came; and standing outside they sent to him and called him. And a crowd was sitting about him; and they said to him, "Your mother and your brothers are outside, asking for you." And he replied, "Who are my mother and brothers?" And looking around on those who sat about him he said, "Here are my mother and my brothers. Whoever does the will of God is my brother, and sister and mother."	While he was still speaking to the people, behold, his mother and his brothers stood outside, asking to speak to him. But he replied to the man who told him, "Who is my mother, and who are my brothers?" And stretching his hand toward his disciples, he said, "Here are my mother and my brothers! For whoever does the will of my Father in heaven is my brother, and sister, and mother."

Examining the details of the two stories we find some differences that make Matthew's account seem much milder. In Mark, Mary and the brethren are using the family authority to call him away and seize him (in view of 3:21). In Matthew, they are only *desirous* to speak with him, which could be quite understandable as family members. In Mark, a strong contrast emerges between those outside (repeated twice) and those inside—the disciples. Jesus turns and looks around at his disciples, as if to make a definite contrast. In Matthew, Jesus only stretches his hand toward the disciples and says, "Here is my mother and my brethren." This new family of Jesus is not set in definite contrast to his own mother, brother and sisters, but could also include them as well.

The story of Jesus' rejection at Nazareth is likewise much gentler in tone toward Jesus' family. After Jesus spoke in Nazareth his home town on a Sabbath, many were astonished, and some took offense at him. In Mark 6:4, Jesus replied, "A prophet is not without honor, except in his own country, and among his own kin, and in his own house." However Matthew 13:57 omits the words, "among his own kin." This is due to Matthew' elevated view of Jesus' family, especially his mother. The story concludes in Mark with the note,

> Indeed he could do no mighty work there, except that he laid his hands upon a few sick people there and healed them. And he marvelled because of their unbelief.

Notice the much milder ending of the same story in Matthew: "And he did not do mighty works there because of their unbelief." (13:58)

CONCLUSION

Mary's virginal conception of Jesus by the Holy Spirit is the unique way Matthew teaches that Jesus is truly Messiah and Son of God from birth. For Matthew it was extremely important to find this in God's eternal plan hidden in the Scriptures where Isaiah the prophet had a vision of a future mother bringing forth a great king of the Davidic dynasty who would be a sign of God's presence in his people even though it all seemed impossible. Despite the fact that Mary has already been dead many years when this gospel was written, the image of a Virgin-Mother and child is a precious and permanent one for the author and his community.

The sign of mother and child teaches forever who God is—a loving God, God of history, faithful to his promises despite every human obstacle as he works through a woman to bring the Messiah, the Son of God and a new age into the world. The same image teaches also who Jesus is: the unique Son of God because only God as Father could make possible the birth of such a son through a virgin mother. Matthew gives us little information on the person and character of Mary. This must wait for the gospel of Luke.

4

The Laughing Virgin:
Mary, Model and Mother
of Believers in Luke
Part I

Although Matthew presented us with the mother-child image as a sign of God's plan, we have learned very little about Mary as a human person. Luke will change all this and provide a striking new image of Jesus' mother in Christian community. What accounts for Luke's unusual interest in Mary and the extraordinary portrait of her that will emerge from his gospel?

An important guide to research is the increased scholarly consensus on the unity of Luke-Acts.[10] Problems mentioned in Acts will reverberate in the gospel. Within Acts, the city of Ephesus draws a major share of the author's attention. Paul, the hero of Luke's narrative, spent three years working there (20:31). Luke appears very concerned about "errors" in this city: he notes that Paul called together the presbyters of Ephesus to warn them against false teachers (20:17-35, esp. 29, 30). Also, Luke provides a detailed description of opposition and a riot on the part of silversmiths and followers of Artemis, the great mother-goddess whose central

---

[10]Cf. especially O'Toole.

shrine was in that city (19:23-41).

We do not know all the false teachings that Paul warned the presbyters of Ephesus about, but we do have definite indications about one group: followers of John the Baptist. These were "Christians" who knew about Jesus but did not have developed beliefs about him. One of these, Apollos, is described as someone versed in the scriptures and the way of the Lord, with accurate information about Jesus, but knowing only the baptism of John. Later, when Paul came to Ephesus, he found "disciples" who were baptized by John but without knowledge or experience of the Holy Spirit (19:1-7). In both cases above, further initiation or instruction was required (18:26; 19:4-5).

Scholars have recognized[11] that Luke's gospel takes special care to present Jesus in a superior light to John. The Baptist's followers had certainly emphasized the unusual character and mission of their master. There are some indications in Mark and Matthew that the Baptist was considered by some as an Elijah *redivivus*: he wears the typical garb of Elijah (Matt. 3:4; Mark 1:6); he appears with Jesus and Moses in the transfiguration scene (Matt. 17:4; Mark 9:4). After this event the disciples asked Jesus about Elijah. In response Jesus explained to them that Elijah had already come but that people did to him as they pleased (Mark 9:13). This hint about John the Baptist becomes more explicit in Matthew's version, where he notes that Jesus was speaking to them about John the Baptist.

These beliefs about the Baptist as a returned Elijah originated in Jewish legends that Elijah, in being brought to heaven in a fiery chariot, (2 Kings 2:1, 11, 12) did not really die but was being kept in heaven until a special time appointed by God. Thus the prophet Malachi affirmed that God would send Elijah before the great and terrible day of the Lord in order to turn the hearts of the people to God (4:5). The same belief is reflected in Sirach 48:9-11. It is found also in 2 Chronicles 21:12-15 in the form of a

[11]Cf. LaVerdiere, pp. 18-20 for a summary of this view.

mysterious letter written by the apparently dead Elijah to Joram the king. In New Testament times, the Jewish historian Josephus relates that Elijah mysteriously "disappeared and that no one knows of his death to this day" (Antiq. IX, 2.2).

These legends about Elijah and his return must have been very important for the Baptist's disciples in arguing the unique position of the Baptist vis-a-vis Jesus. Accordingly, Luke takes definite steps to counter this tendency. Luke omits the reference to John the Baptist's clothes that make him resemble Elijah (Mark 1:6). Luke records a specific denial by the Baptist the he was the Messiah (3:15-17). Luke also omits the story of the Baptist's death (Mark 6:14-29; Matt. 14:1-12), perhaps because the death of a martyr and prophet was too much like Jesus' death. Again, the fact that the Baptist's disciples were the source of the story (Matt. 14:12) also may have induced Luke to suppress it. In the sequel to the Transfiguration story (9:28-36), Luke also omits the question about Elijah and his identification with John the Baptist.

The question of the Baptist's origin is also a special concern of Luke. John's disciples no doubt pointed to the Baptist's priority to Jesus and his mysterious origins— perhaps as a returned Elijah—as signs of his superiority to Jesus. In response, Luke makes a striking contrast between the annunciation and birth accounts of both Jesus and the Baptist. On this there is no need to elaborate because of the considerable past work of scholars.[12] Perhaps the very fact that Luke contains such stories is a way to "bring the Baptist down to earth" and counter legends of a mysterious "re-incarnation" of a heavenly Elijah. Yet it is not certain[13] whether Luke has introduced such stories or whether he has obtained them from Baptist circles.

In demonstrating the superiority of Jesus over the Baptist, it was supremely important for Luke to show that Jesus'

---

[12]Beginning with Laurentin and emphasized by LaVerdiere.

[13]Cf. Brown, pp. 244-50 for a discussion and bibliography.

conception and birth were more extraordinary than that of the Baptist. Even the gospels themselves regard the birth of John the Baptist as among the greatest of human history. Both Matthew and Luke retain Jesus' saying from their common "Q" source that states, "Among those born of women there has risen no one greater than John the Baptist" (Matt. 11:11; Luke 7:28). By "Q" we mean the texts common to Matthew and Luke, but not in Mark, that have prompted many scholars to posit an earlier documentary source.

Of all the human births in the Old Testament, that of Isaac to Abraham and Sarah in their old age is surely the most unusual (Gen. 21:1-2). Even without a careful study of details, the story of the annunciation and birth of the Baptist is remarkably similar to those about Isaac from Abraham and Sarah. Elizabeth and Zechariah (the Baptist's parents) are childless and advanced in age. In each case God sends news of the coming birth (Gen. 18:10, 14; Luke 1:17). Both Abraham and Zechariah hesitate, saying "how shall I know this?" (Gen. 15:7; Luke 1:18). Elizabeth's joy in conceiving a child in her old age is very much like that of Sarah (Gen. 21:6-7; Luke 1:57-58).

However, Luke wants to show that Jesus' birth and annunciation far surpasses that of John. He does this in several ways. For example, Zechariah remains obstinate in his hesitation on receiving the extraordinary news, but Abraham ultimately believes and is rewarded by God. While Elizabeth is advanced in years, it is not specifically mentioned, as with Sarah, that she no longer had her womanly periods (Gen. 18:11). The second way Luke does this is by describing Jesus' mother as even surpassing Sarah, the mother of Isaac.

Luke emphasizes Sarah, rather than both Abraham and Sarah because the stories in Genesis 17 and 22 single her out in an unusual way. No miraculous action seems to be needed in regard to Abraham. Although 86 years of age (16:16), he is well able to sire a child through Hagar the handmaid of Sarah. Even after the death of Sarah (at 117, cf. Gen. 17:15; 23:1), Abraham marries Keturah and has six more children

(25:1). In addition, God gives Sarah a new name, in view of the special divine action through her. She is the only woman in the O.T. to be given that privilege (17:5). She also receives a special blessing from God and is told that she will be the mother of nations: "I will bless her, and moreover I will give you a son by her; I will bless her and she shall be a mother of nations" (17:16). Because the miraculous birth will be only possible through God's intervention, God's part seems more stressed than Abraham's: "I will give you a son through her." This same idea is repeated in 18:9, 14; 21:1. Completing the unusual picture of Sarah is the fact that she is among the few women directly spoken to by God (18:14) and the only one whose age at death is given (23:1).

THE MODEL OF SARAH AND LUKE'S PORTRAIT OF MARY AS MOTHER OF BELIEVERS

The following are the texts where we find indications that Luke has made use of a Sarah-Mary parallel in order to show that the conception of Jesus is equal to or greater than that of the Baptist. Not all are of equal force; some may be only allusions. However, the sum-total, I believe, will amount to a persuasive argument.

1) The sixth month reference in 1:26, 37. The Book of Jubilees[14] relates that the Lord visited Sarah in the sixth month as he had promised. The repetition of sixth month in Luke 1:26, 37 and the leading up "five months" in 1:25 seem to indicate that the author considers the "sixth month" very significant.

2) The new name. Sarah, as we noted, is the only O.T. woman given a new name by God. Audet[15] has provided support to believe that Luke is describing the conferral of a new name, *Kecharitōmenē* (favored one," 1:28) on Mary. Audet noted the typical biblical process in such a matter: the new name, and then the explanation of the meaning of the

---

[14]Jubilees, 16:12.
[15]Cf. bibliog.

name. In this case, the new name means it is someone who has found grace with God (1:30). The fact that the angel calls her by her actual name "Mary" following her hesitation would seem to indicate a connection between new and old names; i.e., "It is you, Mary, that I am greeting with the name *Kecharitōmenē.*" If the name parallel is true, Mary is the only other woman, like Sarah, given a new name directly by God (through an angel).

3) *Kecharitōmenē* and the legend of Sarah's extraordinary beauty. This Greek word is capable of a double meaning referring either to external beauty or more internal "grace." Mary appears to misunderstand or be confused about it. "She was troubled by this word, *epi tou logou* and wondered what this greeting could mean" (1:29). The angel assures her that it means she has found favor with God (1:31). Mary's confusion and fright may have been in regard to the first meaning of the greeting which could mean external beauty or grace. It is found in this sense in Sirach 18:17, in Psalm 17:26, and in some Greek manuscripts of Sirach 9:8, where there is question of being led astray by a beautiful woman. This meaning in reference to beauty has stayed alive in the Greek language, where *kecharitōmenē* can still mean a very beautiful woman in modern Greek dictionaries and usage.[16]

The meaning of "beauty" may have special significance if Luke has in mind the biblical portrait of Sarah who is described as a very beautiful woman even in her old age in Gen. 12:11, 14, 15. As time goes on, this legendary beauty increases. The Greek O.T. heightens it. The Genesis apocryphon fragment of the Dead Sea scroll has a long description[17] of Sarah's physical beauty. Later on, in the first century, the Jewish historian Josephus praises Sarah as the most beautiful of all women (Antiq. I.8.1).

Thus Luke may be pointing out that Mary surpasses Sarah in beauty, since she has the interior beauty of one who

---

[16]Cf. Cole, article in bibliography for a study of the linguistic double meaning of inner or external beauty.

[17]In the beginning of chap. XX. Cf., J. Fitzmyer, Bibliog.

has found favor with God. A similar contrast between inner and external beauty seems also brought out in the text where Noah likewise finds favor with God (Gen. 6:8) in contrast with the "sons of God" in 6:2 who were led astray by the external beauty of the daughters of men. The contrast between women's inner and outer beauty is also known elsewhere in the N.T. (1 Peter 3:3-4), where Sarah is mentioned as an example for imitation in obedience.

4) Mary the Virgin, Sarah and Rebekah. The key miracle text about Sarah's conception of Isaac is that of Gen. 18:11 where it is stated (literally) "It was no longer with Sarah according to the custom of women." Philo of Alexandria, in his allegorical interpretation[18] is very much taken up with this text. He calls Sarah a virgin *(parthenos)*. While we have no evidence that Luke read or knew Philo, the thinking process of an educated hellenistic Jew is valuable as a clue to Luke's process also. Philo, however, finds Rebekah superior as "always a virgin."

Luke, as we have seen, is concerned to show Mary's conception is equal to if not superior to that of Sarah. Yet while Sarah was a married woman when chosen to bear the promised son, Rebekah the future mother of Jacob/Israel was still an unmarried virgin when chosen to be the wife of Isaac (and bearer of the promises) by a special sign (Gen. 24:12-27). In this way, Rebekah is very much like Mary, whose virginity is three times mentioned (1:26, 27, 34). A remarkable textual coincidence indicates a likelihood that Luke had this text in mind. Not only is Rebekah specifically called a virgin, *parthenos*, but also more explicitly "she did not know man" (Gen 24:16). The same expression in the first person is found in Luke 1:34, where Mary asks about how it will all happen, using the words, "Since I do not know man," confirming the meaning of *parthenos* in 1:27, 28. The coupling of *parthenos* and this expression is unique in the bible occurring only here and in Gen. 24:16 in regard to Rebekah. In addition, the poles of inner and outer beauty

[18]In *de Cherubim* 49, de posteritate Caini, 134.

are also in Gen. 24:13-27, as in Mary's annunciation. Rebekah is described as "very beautiful" (24:16). Yet Abraham's servant prays to God for a sign to point out a woman of extraordinary inner beauty and generosity—a woman who will not only offer him water to drink but will also take upon herself the enormous task of watering ten thirsty camels also (Gen. 24:12-14; 17-21).

In connection with the virginity of Mary it has been said[19] that the text of Isaiah 7:14, "A virgin (LXX) will conceive, etc." is behind the angel's words to Mary, "You are to conceive, and bear a son, and you will name him Jesus" (1:30-31). The sequence of conceiving, bearing and naming is in both texts, while the mention of *parthenos* is in Isaiah as well as Luke 1:26-27. Matthew, of course, connects the virginal conception with Isaiah 7:14 by a direct quotation (1:23). However, in Luke there appears no explicit connection. The sequence of conceiving, bearing, naming is found in other O.T. texts, e.g. in regard to Hagar (Gen. 16:22). The connections to Sarah and Rebekah appear to be a better biblical model for a virginal conception than the Isaian text.

5) "How shall I know this?" Abraham also says "how shall I know" in asking for a sign (Gen. 15:8) and so does Zechariah (1:18). Sarah asks for no sign but does laugh in astonishment (18:12, 13, 14, 15). By a nuance, Luke shows that Mary's reaction of faith is superior to Abraham, Zechariah and Sarah. Mary asks, "How shall this take place?" (1:34). These words seem only a request to know how conception can occur in a virgin; they are not a hesitating demand for a sign. Later Elizabeth praises Mary for her faith in believing the divine promises (1:45). However, the sign Mary does not demand is freely given to her by the angel, who announces that Mary's cousin Elizabeth has conceived in her old age. Thus, Mary's question fits into the whole theme of superiority to Abraham, Sarah and Zechariah. The extraordinary birth of the Baptist is even a sign of

---

[19]Cf. Brown, *The Birth of the Messiah*, p. 299.

a coming greater birth to take place.

6) "The Holy Spirit will come upon you" (1:35). The text points to God as the sole cooperative agent in the conception of the child. This is once again similar but beyond the unique action of God in Sarah affirmed by the statement, "I will give you a son by her" (Gen. 18:15). As already pointed out, Abraham had no need of a miracle on his part; the miraculous action is in Sarah. Consequently the texts emphasize the cooperation of God and Sarah, culminating with the statement that God visited Sarah and did as he had promised (21:1). In regard to Mary, the result of this unprecedented cooperation of God with a woman is the birth of a child who can be called Son of God (1:35).

7) The laughing Sarah and the laughing virgin: "Nothing is impossible with God" (1:37). This phrase is also found in Gen. 18:14 as God's reply to Sarah's skeptical laughter which is mentioned four times (18:12, 13, 14). This laughter theme is taken up again in the birth of Isaac—meaning laughter. The skeptical laughter is now turned into a laughter of joy as Sarah exclaims, "God has made me laugh, and all those who hear of it will laugh with me" (Gen. 21:6). In Mary's annunciation, Sarah's skeptical laughter becomes the joyful laughter of the surprised virgin. This joy is underlined in Mary's haste to visit her cousin Elizabeth where the child in Elizabeth's womb leaps for joy. In response, Mary expresses her joy in a canticle of thanksgiving (1:39-56).

"Behold the handmaid of the Lord; let it be to me according to your word" (1:38). This also recalls the Sarah story, where the miraculous conception of Sarah is related in these words, The *Lord* visited Sarah and (literally) *did to her according to his word.* (Gen. 21:1)

8) "Blessed are you among women, and blessed is the fruit of your womb ... blessed is she who has believed that (or because) the things promised her by the Lord will be fulfilled" (1:45). In the O.T., Sarah is the only woman to receive a blessing directly from God—indeed a double one (Gen. 17:15). Mary again parallels her as the Holy Spirit (1:41) prompts Elizabeth to bestow a double blessing on

Mary. The first blessing is in view of the child of promise within her and the second is because of her faith. In the O.T., one who is blessed by God brings blessings to others. This is brought out by God's blessing on Abram in Gen. 12:1-2 where Abram's name (person) becomes a source of blessing for others. Sarah's blessing continues on to others as "nations come out of her" (17:16). Likewise, Mary exclaims that all generations will call her blessed (1:48). Mary's greeting (a form of blessing) also brings a very prized favor to Elizabeth with a sudden jump (Greek word for "dance") of the child in her womb (1:44).

The second type of blessing in view of faith is found implicitly in the Sarah story, but directly in regard to Abram, where it may include Sarah as well: "Abram believed and it was credited to him as justice" (Gen. 15:6). However, there is elsewhere evidence of a tradition in the N.T. about Sarah's faith and her example as a mother of believers which Luke may have drawn upon. Paul speaks of Sarah as Abraham's "freeborn wife" (Gal. 4:22) and refers to Christians as children of the free born wife (4:31). This free born woman is also called Jerusalem from above which is free and our mother (4:26). The letter to the Hebrews declares that it was by faith that Sarah was able to conceive because she believed that God would be faithful to his promises (11:11-12). The First Letter of Peter echoes Galatians in presenting Sarah as a mother to be imitated, especially in regard to obedience: "You are now her children as long as you live good lives" (3:5-7).

CONCLUSION AND CONSEQUENCE

Luke's model of Sarah the great mother of the Jewish people prepares the way for a new Christian understanding of Mary. She is not only Jesus' mother, but the model of all believers because of her faith in God's promises despite impossible circumstances. Like Sarah of old, Mary is the carrier of blessings for her children, first to Elizabeth, then to John the Baptist in his mother's womb and then to Christian believers. The praise and blessings bestowed on her by God (through an angel) and Elizabeth (inspired by the Holy Spirit) seem meant to continue ("all generations shall call me blessed"), since it is the Holy Spirit who was behind them.

The Remembering Mother: A Source of Continuity and Succession in the Christian Community

FURTHER PROBLEMS FOR LUKE AND HIS COMMUNITIES

In addition to the specific problem about the Baptist at Ephesus, there were other serious questions Luke wished to answer in his twofold world. Robert Karris[20] has presented good arguments that our author was concerned about the historical continuity of the Jesus movement and the justification for a Gentile apostolate. We find these concerns in Luke's last chapter. As for historical continuity, the physical reality of the risen Jesus was questioned by some. When Jesus appeared to the gathered disciples, Luke writes, "They were startled and supposed they had seen a spirit" (24:37). Jesus has to assure them by inviting them to touch him and see the marks of his crucifixion. When doubts persist, he even ate a piece of broiled fish in their presence (24:39-43). These questions reflect concerns of Luke's audience many years after the events.

Following this, Jesus deals with the question of historical continuity and an apostolate to the whole world. He explains that all that has happened so far, even his tragic death, is part of a secret divine plan hidden in the Scriptures to bring repentance and forgiveness to the whole world. In his final words, Jesus says, "These are my words which I spoke to you, while I was still with you, that everything written about me in the law of Moses and the prophets must be fulfilled"

[20]Cf. bibliog.

(24:44). Then follows the outline of this divine plan:

> Then he opened their minds to understand the scriptures and said to them, "Thus it is written, that the Christ should suffer and on the third day rise from the dead and that repentance and forgiveness of sins should be preached in his name to all nations, beginning from Jerusalem. (24:45-47)

These words are a link to Luke's second volume, the Acts of the Apostles. This book will show how this divine plan continues at work in the history of the early church. So Jesus' last words in the gospel connect with the beginnings of Acts, where the Holy Spirit (the Spirit of Jesus) will descend on the community to begin a world-wide apostolate. The very last words of Jesus are, "Behold I send the Promise of my Father upon you; but stay in the city, until you are clothed with power from on high (24:59).

We will better understand these Lukan problems of historical continuity and succession (as well as his role for Mary) if we indicate how these problems arose. Scholars, especially C. Talbert[21] have shown that Luke is trying to counteract a growing gnostic or pre-gnostic movement among Christians. Characteristic of such views were a de-emphasis on history and a belief that the expected end time was already completely present through the resurrection and ascension of Jesus. Consequently there would be no coming end of history. The future was now in the present moment. Such a view seems reflected in the question of the disciples to the risen Lord in Acts 1:6, "Lord, will you at this time restore the kingdom to Israel?" Jesus answered them, "It is not for you to know times or seasons which the Father has fixed by his own authority." The disciples are then told by Jesus that they will receive the power of the Holy Spirit and become his witnesses in Jerusalem, Judea, Samaria, and even the ends of the earth. In other words, the Ascension is not the end

---

[21]Cf. bibliog. These paragraphs sum up some of his findings.

time of history. It will be followed by the gift of the Holy Spirit and a time span that will allow the gospel to be carried to the whole world.

According to Luke, it is only after this definite period of time that the return of Jesus and the new era will begin. Our author alludes to this through the words of the two men dressed in white robes who witness the ascension, along with Jesus' disciples. The men say to the disciples,

> Men of Galilee, why do you stand looking into heaven? This Jesus who was taken up from you into heaven, will come in the same way as you saw him go into heaven. (Acts 1:11)

In other words, the disciples are not to consider the ascension of Jesus as an end-point to be "looked at" or contemplated, but as the sign of the beginning of an active mission to the world that must occur before the return of Jesus.

For Luke, the best way to counteract such gnostic tendencies was to emphasize the continuity of God's action in history as stated by the scriptures, which were considered God's own plan for the world. That is why he refers to "the things that have been accomplished among us" in his very first lines of his gospel. The "things that have been accomplished" are God's plan in the Scriptures. This primary Lukan concern has been given special attention by R. Karris[22] and other authors who have closely studied the theology of Luke-Acts. As we noted, the last recorded words of Jesus in Luke's gospel sum up this purpose. The risen Lord opened their minds to understand the Scriptures and find God's plan for his suffering, death and a world apostolate (24:44-47).

Thus, if the stories about Mary are not to be merely peripheral, they must support Luke's central thesis. The idea of a mission to the whole world may sound commonplace to modern readers, but it was a big laugh to a well-educated

---

[22]Cf. bibliog.

person in the Greek world. A Jewish messiah was for those rooted in Jewish history and expectations, and had no more meaning to the rest of the world than a Russian messiah born in Moscow would have to a modern American. Luke, in his Acts, conveys some typical Greek reactions to Paul's speech about a risen Jewish Messiah and world apostolate when he writes, "When they heard of the resurrection of the dead, some mocked; but others said, 'We will hear you again about this'" (18:32).

MARY AND THE REALITY OF JESUS' BIRTH, RESURRECTION, AND CONTINUED PRESENCE

We have seen that the human reality of Jesus' resurrection was a problem for some of Luke's audience in light of chapter 24 and the doubts whether Jesus was a ghost of some kind (24:37). This accords with gnostic tendencies[23] to discount, or even deny, the reality of Jesus' humanity, especially his suffering and death. Luke also had to respond to the question as to whether it was the same human Jesus who died on the cross and rose again. These questions appear to be connected with the nature of the breaking of bread or celebration of the Lord's supper in the early church. We say this because the doubting incident in Luke 24 immediately follows the disciples' recognition of Jesus in the breaking of bread (24:31, 35). The double mention indicates its importance for Luke. On a following page, we will note how Luke's Acts brings out the significance of the breaking of bread in the early church.

In this essential matter of Jesus' true humanity during his earthly life and after, Luke selects Mary as a key witness. Who more than a mother could better affirm the utter weak humanness of a child, especially a newly-born? Consequently, Luke carefully describes Jesus' birth from a human mother: "She gave birth to her first-born son and wrapped him in

---

[23]A description of gnostic characteristics may be found in the introduction to Robinson's Nag Hammadi Library.

swaddling cloths." (2:7) The swaddling cloths are mentioned again in verse 12 where the shepherds also see that the child is thoroughly human, wrapped in swaddling cloths like any other child because of his helplessness. In the O.T. book of Wisdom, Solomon speaks of his birth and being wrapped with swaddling cloths as an indication that he was an ordinary human being: "In swaddling cloths and with constant care I was nurtured. No king has a different birth or origin. All have the same entry into life and all leave it in the same way" (7:4-6).

The connection between swaddling cloths and the sign of the manger (2:12) appears significant. They are also mentioned together in 2:7, and the manger is named a third time in 2:16 along with Mary and Joseph. C. Giblin[24] has pointed out the connection between the manger sign and Isaiah 1:1-2 where the prophet announces that the ox and the ass know where the manger of their Lord is, but Israel does not know him. A manger is a feeding place. The child lying in a place for feeding is a sign that he is indeed the bread or nourishment for his people. This motif of bread is central to Luke. All his gospel, with the frequent meals of Jesus with sinners, tax collectors, pharisees, and his banquet parables lead up to the last supper banquet in chapter 22. After Jesus' resurrection, the same theme continues with the recognition of Jesus at the breaking of the bread by the two disciples who had been on their way to Emmaus (24:28-32).

The eucharistic connection is strengthened by Luke's literary parallel between beginning and end. Mary and Joseph come as strangers to Bethlehem looking for a place to stay. They find no place, and consequently the child is born and laid in a manger, "because there was no room for them at the inn" (2:7) At the end of the gospel, two disciples meet a mysterious stranger, listen to him and offer him hospitality. As a consequence, Jesus manifests himself to them during the breaking of bread. Thus we have a eucharistic allusion at the birth of Jesus as the child lies in a

[24]Cf. bibliog.

feeding place and also after his death when he is found by his disciples in connection with bread and nourishment.

As a result, Mary's witness to Jesus' humanity has significance for the meaning of bread-breaking in the early church. For Luke, this breaking of bread was of central importance. It was one of the distinctive ways that early Christians met together (Acts 2:46). Peter affirmed that he and chosen witnesses ate and drank with Jesus after his resurrection (10:41). In Acts 20:7-12, believers gathered together on the first day of the week to break bread. Paul spoke to them at length and broke bread with them. Mary is thus not only a witness of the truly human birth of Jesus, but also of Jesus' role as bread and nourishment for the world.

Other texts in Luke's infancy story confirm this human portrait. Jesus is circumcised the eighth day like any other child (2:21); presented in the Temple according to the Law (2:27); grew up as a child in his parents' home (2:40); lost at the age of twelve in the Temple; returns home, continues to grow in his Nazareth home until manhood (2:52).

In connection with Jesus' true humanity, it was supremely important for Luke to emphasize the reality of Jesus' death. This also would be very important for eucharistic teaching. For this reason, Luke's account of the Last Supper connects it strongly to Jesus' death. This appears in the emphasis on the cup of suffering twice mentioned in the longer Greek form of Luke's institution narrative (22:14-20). It is also brought out by the introductory remarks of Jesus in which he tells the disciples that he has looked forward to eating the passover with them before he dies (22:15-17).

In reference to Jesus' death, only John's gospel explicitly has Mary as a witness. Luke leaves it a possibility by noting, "All his acquaintances and the women" were by the cross at a distance (23:49). However, Mary's awareness of Jesus' death (and resurrection) appears to be woven into the childhood story of the loss and finding of the twelve year old boy Jesus in the Temple. Luke seems to parallel this story with the end of his gospel. The three days loss occurs in both stories (2:46; 24:21) as well as the day's journey away from

Jerusalem and return (2:44; 24:13, 29, 33). For a mother, even the temporary loss of a child brings worry about death. This childhood incident foreshadows, and from Luke's vantage point looks back to the death of Jesus. Just as the child Jesus is found in the earthly Temple, the risen Jesus is found in the heavenly Temple to which he ascends (24:51-52). Thus Luke presents Mary as a remembering mother, the most effective witness of the reality of Jesus' death.

5

The Laughing Virgin: Mary, Model and Mother of Believers in Luke, Part II

SUCCESSION PROBLEMS AND THE CONTINUING WITNESS OF JESUS' MOTHER

Most important of all, Jesus' mother is witness of the transition from death to life and the continuity of Jesus' presence in the church. To appreciate this, it is necessary to understand how Luke views Jesus' risen life. The modern reader usually distinguishes between Jesus' earthly life and his risen, heavenly life. However, Luke's viewpoint is quite different. One of the great problems he addresses in his two-volume work is that of continuity and succession. As we have seen, there were some Christians who believed that the kingdom had reached its apex with the ascension of Christ. This meant that history was complete and that only an interior awakening to this reality was needed. Consequently, Luke is anxious to point out that the very same human yet divine Jesus was at work both in his earthly life and in the early church.

R. O'Toole[25] has placed special emphasis on this theme of

25esp. pp. 62-86.

continuity. The very same Jesus who walked on earth, taught his disciples, healed and touched people was the one present to the early church and Luke's communities. Thus Jesus as risen Lord was present in eucharistic gatherings (24:31-35), in the preaching of witnesses (Acts 3:22-23; 18:5-11; 26:23), through visions (Acts 7:55-56; 9:1-9), signs and wonders (Acts 4:29-30), through the Holy Spirit (Luke 24:49; Acts 1:2, 8; 2:33, 38, 39; 16:7), and through his powerful name (Acts 2:21, 38; 3:6, 16).

The succession theme is also given great attention by Luke. To confirm Jesus' continued presence, Luke at Pentecost carefully gives the name of each of the twelve (1:13) to establish the link between the earthly life of Jesus and his life in the church. Peter and John speak in Jesus' own name (4:5-22; 5:15-16), even raising the dead (9:32-42). Later, Paul will do the same (14:8-10; 16:16-18; 19:11-12; 20:7-10). Within this succession motif, Jesus' mother plays a key role. She along with other members of Jesus' family are present in Jerusalem as the community awaits and prays for the coming of the Spirit, which is really a return of Jesus: "All these with one accord devoted themselves to prayer, together with the women, and Mary the mother of Jesus and with his brothers." (1:14)

The description of Mary at the first Pentecost was not a time-bound chronological indication. More likely, Luke was presenting a type or model of community gatherings. There were many other "Pentecosts" in Acts. The first was essentially a Jewish Pentecost. Later, the Spirit fell on a Jewish-Gentile audience after Peter's preaching (10:44-46). At Ephesus there was another "Pentecost" as the Spirit descended upon followers of the Baptist after Paul's instruction (19:6-7). After Peter's release there was also a Spirit manifestation as the community gathered together in thanksgiving: "And when they had prayed, the place where they gathered together was shaken; and they were all filled with the Holy Spirit" (4:31).

The timeless nature of Pentecost, with Mary's presence, becomes more certain when we remember that Mary had long been dead by the time Luke finished his two-volume work. Yet she is pictured as associated with and praying with the community of believers. Thus we have a remarkable picture of continuity and succession. Not only is the same Jesus present, but his mother also, in what appears to be an intercessory role.

THE BLESSING OF ABRAHAM AND THE "BLESSED AMONG WOMEN"

We have noted that Luke closes his gospel with Jesus' prediction of a world apostolate as part of the divine plan. Where would such a plan be found? It certainly could not have been accidental or haphazard; it must be in God's mind from the origins of Israel, from the time of Abraham and Sarah their great father and mother. Luke found that the story of Abraham's call indeed contained the perspective of a world-wide plan. The Lord said to Abraham,

> Go from your own country and your kindred and your Father's house to the land that I will show you. And I will make of you a great nation, and I will bless you, and make your name great so that you will be a blessing. I will bless those who bless you, and him who curses you I will curse; and in you *all the families of the earth will be blessed.* (Gen. 12:1-3)

This promise to Abraham appears to be very much on Luke's mind. We have already noted the similarities between the birth of Isaac (from Sarah and Abraham) and the birth of Jesus from Mary. In addition, Luke specifically refers to God's promises to Abraham. In her joyful song of thanksgiving, Mary exclaims,

> He has helped his servant Israel, in remembrance of his mercy, as he spoke to our fathers, to Abraham and to his posterity for ever. (2:55)

For Luke, Jesus is this chosen offspring, the bearer of blessings to the whole world. The last verses of the gospel describe Jesus ascending into heaven and blessing his people:

> Then he led them out as far as Bethany, and lifting up his hands he blessed them. While he blessed them, he parted from them and was carried up into heaven. (24:50-51)

This blessing action is a continual one from heaven as the church continues Jesus' mission to the world. In the Temple, Peter addressed the people with these words:

> You are the sons of the prophets and of the covenant which God gave to your fathers, saying to Abraham, "And in your posterity shall the families of the earth be blessed." God having raised up his servant, sent him to you first, to *bless* you in turning every one of you from your wickedness. (Acts 3:25-26)

It is significant that Luke connects Mary with the blessing made to Abraham. Because of Mary's inseparable relationship to Jesus in her miraculous conception and nurturing role as mother, she was blessed by the Holy Spirit four times: first, by the message of the Angel (1:28-35), then twice by Elizabeth as the instrument or agent of the Spirit (1:42, 45), finally the prophet Simeon, led by the Spirit into the Temple also blessed her (2:17, 34). These blessings came because she, as the bearer of the promised one, was the fulfillment of the blessing of Abraham, who was told that both he and his offspring would be a source of blessing for the world.

In the bible, those especially blessed by God become a source of blessing to others. God said to Abraham, "I will bless you,... so that you will be a blessing" (12:2). This came to pass even in the earthly life of Abraham. God heard Abraham's prayer for Sodom and Gomorrah and promised to spare it if ten just people could be found (18:32). God spared Abraham's nephew Lot and his daughters because of the patriarch (19:29). Upon Abraham's prayer, God healed Abimelech and his household, enabling them to be fruitful once more (20:17). We have seen that Jesus received the blessing of Abraham and passed it on to others. The same is true of Mary carrying within her the promised offspring. After the angel's annunciation and her conception by the Holy Spirit, she visited her cousin Elizabeth. Her greeting, a form of blessing, had such power that it brought a special grace to her cousin who felt the stirring of the child within her as if it were jumping for joy:

> And when Elizabeth heard the greeting of Mary, the babe leaped in her womb and Elizabeth was filled with the Holy Spirit and she exclaimed with a loud cry, "Blessed are you among women and blessed is the fruit of your womb.... For behold, when the voice of your greeting came to my ears, the babe in my womb leaped for joy." (1:41-45)

When Luke wrote his gospel, we noted that Mary the Mother of Jesus had been dead for many years. Yet Luke did not write from a mere antiquarian interest. He regarded Mary as forever blessed because of her permanent relationship with Jesus. Consequently, these texts seem to tell us that Mary (along with her son) continues to be a source of blessing for the early Christian community. The same Holy Spirit that prompted Elizabeth to praise Mary with a blessing could not possibly change in withdrawing this praise and blessing. Mary's own song of response seems to confirm this when she sings, "All generations will call me blessed." (1:48) Luke could hardly have written these words if blessings and praises of Mary were not a felt reality within his experience in the Christian communities he addressed. It is simply one more way that succession and continuity will be found in the experience and worship of believers.

THE REMEMBERING MOTHER AND GOD'S HIDDEN PLAN BEHIND JESUS' SUFFERING AND DEATH

In the previous section, we saw that Jesus' last words outlined God's plan for the whole world. To accomplish this, Luke pointed to Abraham the father of all believers as a beginning. However, this great divine plan was to be effected only through the scandal of the cross. So Jesus introduced his last statements in the gospel with these words: "Thus it is written, that the Christ should suffer and on the third day rise from the dead" (24:46). These words are so difficult that Luke will show that only the risen Lord can open up the disciples' minds to understand them (24:45, 32). However, this understanding will come only to those who are deeply concerned about these things and ponder over them. This was the case of the two perplexed disciples on the way to Emmaus (24:14-15).

Luke is anxious to portray Mary, Mother of Jesus, as a model for those who remember and ponder over the meaning of God's plan. This role of remembering is extremely important for Luke. On the day of Jesus' resurrection, two men in white robes spoke in this manner to the women who had come to anoint Jesus' body: *Remember* how he told you, while he was still in Galilee, that the Son of Man must be delivered into the hands of sinners, and be crucified, and on the third day rise." Then it is stated, "And they *remembered* his words." (24:6-7)

This remembering role of Mary first appears when Luke describes her reaction to the shepherds' visit and the sign of the manger: "Mary kept all these things, pondering them in her heart" (2:15). This statement can indicate Mary's eyewitness of the events, but Luke is even more concerned about their meaning in God's plan. Luke describes how this plan will cause Mary great suffering. When the child Jesus was presented in the Temple, Simeon, inspired by the Holy Spirit, said to Mary, "A sword will pierce through your own soul also, that thoughts out of many hearts may be revealed" (2:35).

The prediction starts to be fulfilled in the next incident twelve years later when the child Jesus was lost for three days and found in the temple. The sorrow and anguish of the parents on this occasion is reflected in the words of his mother, "Son, why have you treated us so? Behold, your father and I have been looking for you anxiously" (2:48). Jesus' reply reveals the bitter truth that the priority of his relationship with his Father will bring much suffering to them. Jesus answered them, "How is it that you sought me? Did you not know that I must be in my Father's house?" (2:49). Luke records that Jesus' parents did not understand this saying (2:50). But he also notes that Jesus' mother as in 2:15 kept all these things in her heart as a remembering mother (2:51).

Luke draws special attention to the cross in God's plan of salvation through Jesus' three predictions about his suffering, death and resurrection. While Mark and Matthew indicate the mysterious nature of these sayings, Luke underlines the hiddenness and human incomprehensibility more than the other two evangelists. At the end of the second prediction, Matthew simply notes that the disciples were greatly distressed (17:23); Mark writes that they did not understand the saying (9:32). However, Luke adds not only that they did not understand it but that "it was concealed from them, that they should not perceive it" (9:45). In the third prediction, Matthew and Mark note only the actual words of Jesus without the reactions of the disciples (Matt. 20:18; Mark 10:34). Luke, however, adds the following: "They understood none of these things; this saying was hid from them, and they did not grasp what was said" (8:34). Luke emphasizes this hiddenness because of his conviction that God's mysterious plan to save people through the shame of the cross is so completely beyond human minds that it can only be revealed by the risen Jesus (24:25-27, 32, 45).

Luke presents Mary also as not comprehending this aspect of God's saving plan. In Simeon's prophecy and her child's loss in the Temple, it was foreshadowed. Although she did not understand, she did not reject it but pondered over it searching for its meaning. In this way, she is presented as the model for the believer. Despite the fact that the cross presented an apparent end of hope, she waited in Jerusalem (Acts 1:14) for the return and continued presence of her son through his sending of the Spirit at the first Pentecost. Her return to Jerusalem was in obedience to Jesus' word: "Stay in the city until you are clothed with power from on high" (24:59). The Acts of the Apostles opens by recalling this command, by way of added emphasis: "While staying with them, he charged them not to depart from Jerusalem, but to wait for the promise of the Father" (1:4). Thus Mary is among those who believe in Jesus' word about a surprising return despite its human impossibility.

THE TRANSFORMED IMAGE OF MARY IN THE REST OF LUKE'S GOSPEL

Luke 1-2 is a "mini-gospel" summarizing his whole message in the infancy accounts. So we would expect that the image of Mary as mother of believers would be found in the rest of the gospel also. Mary is found there twice, in 8:19-21 and 11:27. In both cases it is in reference to her role as mother. The significance of the first passage may be highlighted by comparisons with Mark and Matthew. In Mark 3:31-35, the story of Mary and the family seeking out Jesus is in a context of opposition. Mark had stated that the crowds surrounding Jesus did not even leave him time to eat, and "when his friends heard about it they went out to seize him, for they said, 'He is beside himself'" (3:21). Following this Mark describes the Scribes who accused Jesus of casting out devils by the chief of devils himself. Finally, Mark writes,

> His mother and his brethren came; and standing outside they sent to him and called him. And a crowd was sitting about him; and they said to him, "Your mother and your brethren are outside, asking for you." (3:31-32)

The passage appears connected to previous details in 3:20 that the surrounding crowds did not even leave Jesus time to eat. This is followed by reactions of literally "those with him," which seems to refer to Jesus' family. The family decides to use its authority to call Jesus out of the house. Jesus' reaction in Mark is by way of sharp contrast. He replies, "Who are my mother and my brethren?" Then, by way of dramatic emphasis he looked around at those seated about and said, "Here are my mother and my brethren! Whoever does the will of God is my brother, and sister, and mother" (3:34-35). There appears to be a similar atmosphere of confrontation when Jesus leaves his home town in Mark 6 and remarks that a prophet is not without honor, except in his own country, and *among his own kin, and in his own house* (6:5).

Here we cannot analyze in detail these statements of apparent hostility in Mark. They may reflect a historical picture in Jesus' own life time when his own family either misunderstood or opposed his preaching mission. This may have been due to the threat to both Jesus and themselves that could come from the Romans or king Herod, if Jesus were suspected to be a messianic pretender. The gospel of John reflects a similar picture when Jesus decided not to go up to the feast of Tabernacles in public, and his brethren pushed him to go. The author records, "Even his brethren did not believe in him" (John 7:5).

When we studied the parallel passage in Matthew, we observed that the incident was somewhat toned down. However, when we look at Luke, we find remarkable differences:

> Then his mother and his brothers came to him, but they could not reach him for the crowd. And he was told, "Your mother and your brothers are standing outside, desiring to see you." But he said to them, "My mother and my brothers are those who hear the word of God and do it." (8:19-21)

We notice immediately that there is no question of using parental or family authority to call Jesus out. In Luke, they simply want to see him and cannot do so on account of the crowds. In contrast to Matthew and Mark, Jesus does not differentiate between family and disciples by asking who is his mother or his brethren. Nor does he heighten any opposition by stretching his hand as in Matthew, or looking around at the disciples as in Mark. He simply states, "My mother and my brothers are those who hear the word of God and do it" (8:21).

In Luke's version, Jesus' mother is not differentiated from or opposed to the disciples; rather, she is included among them not as a mere physical mother of Jesus but as one who is a mother and model in the community because she hears the word of God and keeps it. Luke emphasizes this meaning by placing the story immediately after the parable of the sower where the good soil signifies those who hear with a good heart and bear fruit (8:15). Another difference from the other gospels is found when Luke relates the rejection of Jesus at Nazareth. Jesus states that no prophet is acceptable in his own country (4:25); he omits Matthew and Mark's addition of "in his own house" and (Mark only) "among his own kin."

Why such remarkable differences? Luke must be faithful to his first two chapters, where he painted a strong portrait of Mary as mother of believers. What may have been originally a hostile situation in Jesus' life is no longer important for him. This is because Mary and Jesus' family have been among the early believers after Jesus' death (Acts 1:14), and that is the most important matter for Luke. Consequently, he retells the incident in its new permanent significance. Thus Mary is given her position as true mother in Jesus' continuing community.

The remaining short incident, only in Luke, also reflects this view. As Jesus was speaking one day, a woman in the crowds raised her voice and said to him, "Blessed is the womb that bore you and the breasts that you sucked!" Jesus however replied, "Blessed rather are those who hear the word of God and keep it" (11:27-28). This statement contains the same words as the end of the preceding incident, and parallels the previous sense of meaning: there is no conflict between physical mother and believers, but Mary is to be praised not only as Jesus' mother but as mother of believers.

Mary and the Mother-Goddess Cult at Ephesus

Luke gives considerable coverage to a sharp encounter between Christians and devotees of Artemis, the mother goddess. Ephesus was the center of her cult in the Roman province of Asia. The ancient temple of Artemis at Ephesus was one of the seven wonders of the ancient world. It attracted pilgrims and devotees not only from Roman Asia, but from many parts of Europe as well. The center of attraction was the renowned image of Artemis that the town clerk of Ephesus described in this manner:

> Men of Ephesus, what man is there among you who does not know that the city of Ephesus is the temple-keeper of the great Artemis and the sacred stone that fell from the sky. (Acts 19:35)

The translation "sacred stone" is not certain, but there is no doubt that it refers to the famous revered image of Artemis. Perhaps smaller replicas of this were made by Demetrius and other silversmiths (Acts 19:24). Archaeologists have found statuettes of Artemis distinguished by their fertility symbols featuring dozens of breasts or wheat clusters. No wonder that the craftsmen at Ephesus were disturbed by the growing Christian community and the sharp decline in demand for Artemis' images. Demetrius, the silversmith, gathered together his fellow craftsmen and said to them,

> Men, you know that from this business we have our wealth. And you see and hear that not only at Ephesus but almost throughout all Asia this Paul has persuaded and turned away a considerable company of people

saying that gods made with hands are not gods. (Acts 19:26)

Luke's details confirm the widespread popularity of the mother goddess. Demetrius continues by saying, "There is danger ... that the temple of the great goddess Artemis may count for nothing and that she may even be deposed from her magnificence, she whom all Asia and the world worship" (19:27). The silversmiths then went through the city crying out, "Great is Artemis of the Ephesians," and gathered together a large crowd in the theatre. Luke or his sources must have been shaken by the thunderous ovation the theatre crowd gave to Artemis. For fully two hours they chanted, "Great is Artemis of the Ephesians" (19:34).

It would have been most interesting if Luke provided us some links between the place of Mary, mother of believers and that held formerly by Artemis in the lives of converts. What Luke leaves as a mystery opens the way for at least some speculation. The loss of the deeply loved and revered mother-goddess must have left a great void as the more masculine-centered Christian proclamation won over many converts. While Luke may not have intended it, his presentation of Mary as mother of believers would certainly have found ready acceptance among converts so accustomed to a deep feminine element in their worship and lives.

Perhaps Luke has left us a hint about the relationship between Jesus' mother and mother Artemis. The silversmith story in Acts 19 accentuates the acclamation "great" or "great one" applied to Artemis (19:27, 35) and the two hour chant to her. Elsewhere in Luke, the title "great" is given without qualification only to Mary's future child when the angel tells her, "he shall be *great*, and will be called the Son of the the Most High" (1:32). In contrast, John the Baptist will be "great before the Lord" and Simon the magician is one who *says* that he is some one great (Acts 8:9-10). Because Mary's child will be truly *great*, his mother sings out, "He who is mighty has done great things for me" (1:49). The expression reminds us of the O.T., where only God is described as great, but he does great things in Israel his people (Ps. 126:3). Thus mother and child are placed together by Luke. Mary is "great" through the child she bears, and through the believers who continue to look to her, not only as a model, but as a source of blessing together with her son. This "blessing" may be effected by Mary's activity as an intercessory figure if the scene of Mary praying together with the church in Acts 1:14 is meant to go beyond time limitations and extend to the church at any time.

Mary in Luke: A Summary

Luke has drawn a personal portrait of Mary in response to difficulties and questions arising in Christian communities, especially Ephesus. Responding to an exalted place of John the Baptist, Luke uses the Sarah legend to describe Jesus' even more unusual origin from a virgin who becomes not only mother of Jesus but mother of all believers. Gnostic-influenced teachings tended to discount history, continuity and the reality of Jesus' humanity, especially in his death and risen presence in the Eucharist. In response, Luke presents Jesus' mother as a witness and guarantee of historical continuity and succession. She is also a remembering mother, one who believes the divine promises about Jesus' "impossible" birth. She continues to remember and believe the scriptural plan for Jesus' tragic suffering and death although she does not understand it, at least at first. One of the great obstacles to the growth of Christianity was the widespread popular attachment to the mother goddess in various forms. We can only speculate, with a few hints from Luke that the growing place of Mary as mother of all believers was an important factor during the encounter of a more masculine-centered Christianity with the feminine-dominated fertility cults.

6

The Mother of Jesus:
in the Seven Sign's of John's Gospel[26]

In contrast to Matthew and Luke, there are no birth or infancy accounts in John. This is because Jesus is already the eternal Word of the Father right from the very first verse: "In the beginning was the Word, and the Word was with God, and the Word was God." Instead of Mary's prominent place in the birth accounts of Matthew and Luke, John underlines her role in the beginning of Jesus' public ministry (2:1-12), and likewise at the end, (19:25-37) when Jesus dies on the cross. However, we shall see that this "public ministry" has two levels of meaning. The most important and deeper level concerns the ministry of the risen Jesus in the community. Consequently, the role of Jesus' mother will be understood in view of her place in the life of the church drawing its source from Jesus' death and resurrection.

The investigation of Mary's role in the fourth gospel has given rise to an enormous amount of literature, both in books and articles.[27] In these studies we find a very wide range of interpretation. On one extreme, Mary has been described as practically a third way to God;[28] on the other end of the spectrum, her place has been considered nominal

---

[26]This chapter is drawn from the article of J. Grassi in *CBQ*, cf. bibliog.

[27]Cf. A.M. Serra.

[28]E.g., J. Alfaro.

and almost accidental. Here we wish to present a new approach based on a fresh avenue of investigation. This approach will be based on a study of Mary's role within a suggested restructure of the principal sign narratives of the fourth gospel. It also will keep in mind some of the questions the author wishes to answer in regard to the problems faced by his audience.

THE INTER-RELATION BETWEEN THE WEDDING AT CANA (2:1-12) AND THE OTHER SIGNS

It is almost universally recognized that Mary's role at Cana cannot be understood by itself, but only in relationship to the coming hour of Jesus' death and glorification of which he spoke (2:4). However, relatively little attention has been given to the interlinks between the first sign at Cana of Galilee (2:1-12) and the other signs that follow. Also, the principal signs in John have usually been numbered within the first twelve chapters, with 12:37-50 as a summary proclamation, beginning with the statement, "Though he had done so many signs before them, they did not believe in him." It has been commonly accepted[29] that there are seven principal signs in these chapters: 1) The wedding at Cana (2:1-12); 2) the restoration of the dying son of the royal official (4:46-54); 3) the sabbath healing at the pool of Bethesda (5:1-16); 4) the multiplication of the loaves (6:1-15); 5) Jesus walks on water (6:16-22); 6) the sabbath healing of the blind man (9:1-40) and 7) the restoration of Lazarus to life (11:1-54).

However, M. Girard[30] has brought out persuasive arguments that this is not the arrangement intended by the evangelist. The following is a summary of these arguments: first of all, he accepts R.E. Brown's[31] definition of a sign: a prodigious deed with strong symbolic possibility that illustrates Jesus'

---

[29]E.g., Vawter and R.E. Brown on the fourth gospel.

[30]Cf. bibliog.

[31]The Gospel Acc. to John, p. 527-530.

salvific message. In this regard, sign five above, Jesus' walking on water, does not appear to fit in this category. It seems rather a part of the loaves' total message and meaning, perhaps bringing out a passover context.[32] Secondly, the actual use of the word "sign" in the stories is another indicator. It is found in all the narratives above, but not in Jesus' walk on water. Those places are the following: 2:11; 4:54; 6:1 (referring to the previous healing at Bethesda); 6:14; 9:16; 12:18 (in regard to Lazarus).

However, this leaves us with only six signs. Where is the seventh, if there is one? It would seem strange to leave us with six, like the six incomplete water jars at Cana! To find the seventh sign, there is no compelling reason to conclude the signs with the so-called end of the book of signs in 12:37-50. In fact, the author seems to point to the insufficiency of previous signs, and the necessity of something greater to come. In addition, the author concludes his gospel (if we regard chapter 21 as an appendix) by mentioning signs after the *whole* work of Jesus' death and glorification is complete: "Now Jesus performed many other signs before his disciples, which are not written in this book. . ." (20:30). M. Girard suggests that the seventh sign consists of Jesus' death and the accompanying issue of water and blood from Jesus' side that the disciple finds so extraordinary that he emphasizes that there was (or he was) an eye-witness and that he tells the story so others may believe also (19:35). Thus the first six signs are incomplete and look forward to the seventh at Jesus' great hour of death and glorification when he will be lifted up and draw everyone to himself (12:33). While the word "sign" is not used here, the writer may have considered it appropriate to save it for the conclusion of all these events in 20:30.

A further confirmation of this new seven signs series is found in M. Girard's suggested literary chiastic structure of the seven signs:

---

[32] Jesus passes over the water as God made his people pass over the "Red Sea" at the time of the Exodus, with a possible relation to Ps. 77:20; 78:13.

1) The Wedding Feast at Cana (2:1-12)
  2) The restoration of the dying son (4:46-54)
   3) The sabbath healing at Bethesda (5:1-16)
    4) The multiplication of loaves (6:1-71)
    5) The sabbath healing of the blind man (9:1-41)
  6) The restoration of Lazarus to life (11:1-44)
7) The great hour of Jesus: his mother, the cross, the issue
of blood and water from Jesus' side (19:25-37)[33]

In this structure, we notice immediately some general correspondences: #3 and #5 as sabbath healing signs; #2 and #6 as death to life themes; #1 and #7 complement one another as beginning and end. Linked together are Jesus' mother in both: Jesus' hour (2:4; 19:27), the Cana wine and the bitter wine on the cross (19:29, 30), the imperfect Cana water and the water/blood/Spirit from Christ's side. The sign of the loaves appears in the central part of the gospel. All the signs may contribute to its meaning, especially #1 and #7. Perhaps the numerology, five loaves and two fish with seven as a total yielding twelve left-over loaves hints at the central place among the seven signs held by the loaves sign. Peter's confession at the end of the sign and discourse also supports the central place of #4, the loaves' sign in John's gospel. If it has this central place we would expect common elements with #1 and #7. Examples are the common mention of Jesus' mother (6:42 in most manuscripts); Jesus' blood (6:52, 54; 19:34 and the wine, "blood of the grape" at Cana); the connection to Passover (6:4; 19:31, 2:12, 13); the hour of Jesus' glorification (6:62; 2:4; 19:27).

These structural interconnections can also serve as an important vehicle of meaning in the fourth gospel. This is because the writer often refers to a later event within an earlier one in order to complete its meaning. For example, at the feast of booths, Jesus announced that anyone who

---

[33]The list of the witnesses in 19:25 would be a fitting beginning, followed by the sign itself (the issue of bloody water from Jesus' side), then the faith confession of the beloved disciple and the scripture citations, ending with the looking on the one who was pierced as a possible inclusio.

thirsted should come to him and drink, and that rivers of living water would flow according to the Scriptures (7:37-38). In the next verse, the writer mentions that this will only happen in the future outflow of the Spirit at Jesus' glorification. In the loaves discourse, the evangelist has Jesus say that his flesh and blood are real food and drink (6:55-56), yet this will only be understood in the future ascension of the Son of man to where he came from (6:62-63). Also, the writer brings out that the resurrection of Lazarus is only made possible by the resurrection of Jesus as the source of resurrection and life (11:26). When this present-future link is developed within the literary structural interconnections of the seven signs, it becomes easier for the writer to complete the meaning of Jesus' words and actions in reference to their future completion.

Consequently, if the first and last signs are so closely interconnected with each other and with the loaves' sign, we would expect that they shed meaning on the latter, and perhaps answer some questions or misunderstandings about Jesus' bread found in it. First of all, many people misunderstood the sign and thought it indicated the arrival of a Moses-type prophet into the world. Jesus had to retreat to a mountain fearing they would try to make him a liberator and king (6:13-14). Thus, in terms of bread, some people probably thought of Jesus as a miracle/sign worker, like Moses, who provided Israel with a "wonder bread" (Exod. 16:1-31). In response, Jesus pointed out that Moses did not give them real bread from heaven; it is the Son of Man who will give it to them (6:27). A second question flows from this. If Jesus will give them a heavenly bread as Son of Man, how can this be reconciled with his humanity and obvious family ties with his mother and father? (6:41-42) In other words, can he really have a divine or heavenly origin if his earthly origin is so evident? So "the Jews" rightly ask, "How does he then say, 'I have come down from heaven?'"

A third dispute, a rather heated one, springs up in the audience in response to Jesus' words, "The bread I will give is my flesh for the life of the world" (6:51). Following the view that 6:51-58 specifically pertains to the Eucharist,[34] the audience's reaction would seem to reflect a division[35] in regard to understanding the meaning of the Eucharist in the early church. Some of the people ask, "How can this man give us (his) flesh to eat?" (6:62). Connected with the previous verse, the question would mean, "How can this mere man, flesh and blood, give bread to eat that will be a source of life for the world?" In other words, the humanity of Jesus is a real stumbling block. The problem is so acute that it is presented first as a violent dispute (6:52) and finally as a cause of schism among Jesus' disciples, many of whom abandoned him in view of this teaching (6:60, 66). Jesus replies for the third time that it is the bread of the Son of Man (6:27, 53, 62). However, he adds the explanation that to understand his words they must see the Son of Man ascend to where he was before so they will know that his words are spirit and life, not flesh alone (6:62-63). The promised bread, therefore, is connected with the reality of Jesus' death and glorification, with his ensuing gift of the Spirit.

We can sum up the questions proposed in the fourth sign of the loaves that can be possibly answered in the seventh and first signs: 1) Are the loaves a miraculous wonder bread provided by Jesus, a second Moses and wonder-worker? 2) If the bread is a "bread from heaven," is the Jesus behind this bread really divine, come down from heaven? 3) If so, can he really be human? And connected to this, did he really die? Is his death connected to the Spirit and life associated with the bread fellowship?

---

[34]Here I follow Brown, *The Gospel of John*, p. 284-289. He points out that this section begins with a description of a bread that will be Jesus' flesh for the life of the world. This seems to be built on Jesus' words at the last supper that he would give his bread/life/body/blood/ for others. Verses 51-58 would be a later stage and rethinking of 35-50, with the applications of more precise Eucharistic terminology.

[35]This is suggested by R.E. Brown, *The Community of the Beloved Disciple*, p. 74. Specifically, these would be Jewish Christians who do not not hold John's views of the Eucharist.

The Mother of Jesus in the Seventh Sign (19:25-37)

First of all, we should note that her presence is not incidental, but central in the first and last sign. Her name and presence opens and closes the first sign at Cana, as well as the last[36] sign on the cross. In the first sign, the word "mother" is used four times, and "woman" once; in the seventh sign, "mother" is likewise found four times and "woman" once (19:25, 26, 27).

The seventh sign (19:25-37) begins with the simple statement that the mother of Jesus stood by the cross along with other women. At face value, she would be a most important witness of these central events. The question of historicity (since Mary is not at the cross in the other gospels) need not detain us: the evangelist uses the words "see" and "know" in deeper senses. Even the blind can "see" if they are open to Jesus' words (9:39). A mother, of course, even though not actually present, would have a surer perception and deeper knowledge of the reality and meaning of a son's death than innumerable eyewitnesses. By the time John's gospel was written, the mother of Jesus had probably been dead for many years, yet the author wrote as if the events described were of present significance to his audience (19:35). Perhaps the evangelist understood the scene at the cross not as an event in the past but as a timeless drama. The risen Jesus always bears the marks of the cross and spear wound (20:20, 24). This view is reflected elsewhere in the NT. For example, Paul portrayed Jesus to the Galatians as crucified, although years after the event (3:1).

The words of Jesus to his mother: "Woman, behold your son," and to the beloved disciple, "Behold your mother" are capable of bearing a wide range of meaning, especially in the area of symbolism. In this study, we will limit ourselves to what *she actually does* as a mother in these signs, while

---

[36]In view of note 33, she would be in the *inclusio* of witnesses at the beginning, and those looking upon the pierced one at the end.

recognizing that a wider range[37] of symbolism is possible. It does appear that her role is especially important for the author and his audience; not just a sentimental memory from the past. M. De Goedt[38] has suggested that the words "behold your mother" are a revelatory formula introducing a special new role as a mother, a role she will exercise in regard to the beloved disciple. The words cannot be simply a last enjoinder on Jesus' part that a favorite disciple is to take care of his mother upon his death. They must be understood wiithin the meaning that "the disciple whom Jesus loved" has for this gospel and its audience.

The last word on the identity and meaning of this beloved disciple has not been said and perhaps will never be. The group of twelve scholars whose study and discussions led to the book *Mary in the New Testament*[39] accepted the following as a working hypothesis: 1) that he was a real person thought to have been a companion of Jesus; 2) that he had real significance for the Johannine community, whether or not he was their founder; 3) he is presented as the ideal or model disciple; 4) that he is a very special witness (19:35; 21:24) guaranteeing the community's understanding of Jesus and his teaching. This is very similar to the view held by R.E. Brown in the *Community of the Beloved Disciple*.[40] However, a description of Mary's role in the seventh sign is not contingent on an exact identification of the beloved disciple.

It was very important for the author of the fourth gospel to obtain credibility for his views by establishing a direct link with Jesus. No doubt many Jewish Christians also did so by

---

[37]By what *she actually does*, I do not necessarily mean in a physical, photographic or journalistic sense, but by her understanding of Jesus' death. This understanding is presented by the evangelist in terms of fulfillment of the Scriptures, with Jesus' mother and the beloved disciple as witnesses. Other necessary symbols such as Mary as representing the church or the new Eve may be found in R.E. Brown, Vol. 1, pp. 107-109.

[38]M. De Goedt, p. 142-150. He does this by comparing the seeing, behold and announcement sequence to the scenes in 1:29-34; 1:35-39; 1:47-51.

[39]p. 211.

[40]p. 31.

referring to James, their Jerusalem leader, as the "brother of
the Lord." A succession line of authentic teaching could only
be established by making as close a connection as possible to
Jesus. Consequently, a word of Jesus just before death
confirming a relationship between his mother and the
beloved disciple would be extremely important. It would
establish him as a "brother of the Lord" with authority like
that of James, Jesus' blood relative, and other disciples of
Jesus, even Peter. Thus R.E. Brown writes, "By stressing not
only that his mother has become the mother of the beloved
disciple, but also that the disciple has become her son, the
Johannine Jesus is logically claiming the disciple as his true
brother."[41] P. Minear's study[42] of the beloved disciple,
however, has brought out important Old Testament parallels
of Benjamin as the beloved son of Israel. This invites us to
think of the beloved disciple as a favorite son or protégé of
Jesus, who then continues on as "adopted" by Mary. A
sonship image would seem confirmed by the parallel between
Jesus in the Father's bosom (1:18) and the beloved disciple
reclining on Jesus' bosom (13:25). However, whether in
terms of son or brother, the succession motif would be very
important for the author.

Together, the beloved disciple and Jesus' mother are
associated in witnessing the meaning of the key event in
Jesus' life, sign seven, culminating in the unusual prodigy of
the issue of watery blood from Jesus' side, to which the
evangelist gives special attention. It is important to note
what Jesus' mother actually observes (according to the
author's portrayal), and in *what way* she would act as a
mother. First and foremost, she would be the most important
witness of the utter reality of Jesus' death. As a mother she
felt and knew this more than any other person. It was seared
in her memory for all her life, and known by everyone who
met her. The popular perception of the indelible memory of
a mother for her child is found in Isa. 49:15: "Can a mother

[41]p. 197.
[42]p. 105-123.

forget her infant, be without tenderness for the child of her womb?" Mary would be a mother to the community of the beloved disciple as a carrier of tradition, as one who remembers, which is one of the greatest functions of a mother. Her association with Jesus in any explanation of his person or mission would be a continual reminder of his death and its meaning.

As noted, the question of Jesus' humanity and death would be very important for understanding the central sign of the loaves. The joint witness of Jesus' mother and the beloved disciple would be necessary to answer questions about the flesh and blood reality of Jesus in the loaves' sign, and to explain that it is a bread which the *Son of Man* gives (6:27, 53, 62). This Son of Man in the Eucharistic discourse is portrayed especially in the aspect of exaltation in triumph (6:62). This would go along with the predominant place of the lifting up on the cross in the Son of Man texts of 3:14; 8:28; 12:23, 24. It should also be mentioned that *blood* in the fourth gospel is only found in sign four (6:53, 54, 55, 56) and in sign seven (19:34). (The blood in 1:13 has another sense in reference to the manner of Jesus' birth). In addition, the mother's witness to the humanity of her son in the events of his birth would also be very significant. This is alluded to in the loaves' sign (6:42) where the people's knowledge regarding Jesus' father and mother (in most texts) seems contrary to a statement that Jesus has come down from heaven. However, there is a possibility of a double meaning in the statement about Jesus' father and mother. It is interesting to note that Mary is also seen to be a witness of the reality of Jesus' humanity in a later letter by Ignatius to the Trallians about some who seem to deny this reality (9:1).

Beyond the reality of his death, the gospel has a very special interest in *how Jesus died*. Here is where both the beloved disciple and Jesus' mother are unique witnesses. In presenting this, Jesus' obedience to God's plan as found in the Scriptures is a dominant theme (19:24, 28, 30). Special focus is placed on Psalm 69:21, "In my thirst they gave me bitter wine to drink." The evangelist pictures Jesus very consciously saying "I thirst," and taking the wine in order to fulfill the Scriptures. In addition, as R.E. Brown[43] points out, Jesus obediently accepts the cup of suffering and death in accord with the words at his arrest, "Shall I not drink the cup which the Father has given me?" (18:11) There is special emphasis on this *oxos*, or bitter wine of Psalm 69:21, which is here repeated three times (19:28-30). It is this wine that Jesus takes in obedience. Later we will see in the first sign that Mary will direct the waiters to do everything that Jesus says (2:5). The "good wine" will be made possible through obedience to Jesus' word, just as he has been obedient to the Father on the cross.

Regarding this manner of Jesus' death, a second sign teaching is found in Jesus' supreme control over his death. He knows exactly when he is going to die (19:28); then he says that it is all finished (19:30) and finally he seems to deliberately bow his head and expire. This was anticipated in 10:18, where Jesus said that no one takes away his life from him; he dies by his own choice. He has the power to give (or lay down) his life and take it up again in accord with the command of his Father. This sign points to something supra-human in Jesus' death. It is surely a real death, yet no human being has the power to determine when life will come and when it will go. In the Prologue, the author pointed out that the Word came into the world to be born in the flesh by his own choice; now he dies in the same way. All of this points to a divine element in Jesus. Jesus' mother would be a witness to this, as brought out in the manner Jesus died. For the gospel, this would provide an answer to the question in the loaves sign, "How does he now say, 'I have come down from heaven?'" (6:41) It is significant that immediately after this, in the next verse, Jesus' mother is mentioned. As we noted, there is a possible double meaning or irony in the statement that the audience of Jesus knows about his human origin. It is possible that Jesus' mother does know of his real though mysterious origin.

---

[43] *The Gospel According to John* (xiii-xxi), p. 930.

A third sign teaching witnessed by Jesus' mother concerned the effects of Jesus' death as bringing the promised Spirit to his followers. Of Jesus' death, the evangelist simply wrote, "He bowed his head and gave up the spirit" (19:30). By itself, the phrase means nothing more than that he expired or died. However, in view of the next incident, and Jesus' whole work, the phrase may be proleptic and symbolic of the gift of the Spirit to others. The climactic moment of the seventh sign is the piercing of Jesus' side and the unusual flow of blood and water from his side. The evangelist attaches great import to this; he cites the words of an eyewitness who relates the event so others may believe also (19:35). What does the author see in this event? He does not tell us directly, but we can surmise that it must be connected with some word of Jesus, with the Scriptures, or with both. In regard to the first possibility, Jesus had promised on the last day of the feast of the Tabernacles, "If anyone thirst, let him come (to me, in most texts) and let him drink who believes in me. As the Scripture says 'From within him shall flow rivers of living water'" (7:37-38).[44] This is the translation adopted by R.E. Brown in his commentary on John, where he details his reasons for understanding the second half in regard to Jesus rather than the believer. Regardless of which way it is to be translated, the evangelist in the next verse notes that Jesus was speaking of the Spirit that those who believed in him were to receive, and that this Spirit would only come upon Jesus' glorification. So the surprising flow of bloody water from Jesus' side could be understood as a confirmation of Jesus' words that his glorification on the cross would bring the gift of the Spirit/water as a result of his bloody sacrifice.

A second basis for interpreting the surprise occurrence could be the fulfillment of the Scriptures. The piercing of Jesus' side by the soldiers brought to mind the text (along with its context), "They shall look on him whom they have pierced" (Zech. 12:10, Hebr.). Immediately preceding this we have, "I will pour out on the house of David and on the inhabitants of Jerusalem a spirit of grace and petition." A few verses later, "On that day there shall be open to the house of David and the inhabitants of Jerusalem a fountain to purify from sin and uncleanness" (13:1, Hebr.). Blood was considered especially necessary for purification from sin. So the presence of blood in the flow from Jesus' side would strengthen the application of the text. P. Ellis[45] draws special attention to the actual *flow* of blood, which was considered so important in Jewish Law.

Once again, the links to the fourth sign of the loaves can be noted. In that scene, many disciples refused to accept Jesus' statement about the necessity of eating his flesh and drinking his blood (6:53, 54, 60). As already noted[46] this may refer to Jewish Christians who do not share John's view of the Eucharist. However, Jesus replies that their understanding will be complete when they see the Son of Man ascending and realize that his words are spirit and life (6:62-63). Jesus then openly states that some of them do not believe. The witness of Jesus' mother and the beloved disciple seems to be the fulfillment of Jesus' words: they both see that the exalted Son of Man does indeed provide spirit and life through his death, and thus through the Eucharist. The beloved disciple as a witness sees and believes this along with Jesus' mother (19:35).

The meaning of Passover, and especially the sacrifice of the Passover lamb, is also found within the symbolism of the seventh sign. The first words of the Baptist about Jesus addressed to his disciples (one of whom was probably the beloved disciple, 1:35) were, "Behold the lamb of God who takes away the sin of the world" (1:29). Among the last words about Jesus before his burial, there is a reference to the Passover ritual with the words, "Not a bone of him shall be broken" (Exod. 12:46). This scriptural citation was prompted by another unusual "occurrence" considered as part of a divine plan: The soldiers neglected to break Jesus'

[45]p. 275.
[46]See note 35.

bones, as was ordinarily expected. In not doing so, they allowed Jesus to perfectly parallel the Passover lamb which had to be a whole and entire sacrifice to God, as expected of all sacrifices. Because Jesus drank the bitter "blood of the grape" in obedience, his life/blood became a sacrifice, a prayer offering to God for forgiveness, just as the blood of the Passover lambs sprinkled on Jewish homes saved the people from destruction at the time of the Exodus (Exod. 12:23). This Passover atmosphere is one more link between signs one, four and seven.

Finally, in regard to *how Jesus died*, the role of his mother reached its highest peak in the area of the motivation of his death. This motivation was love for those entrusted to him by his Father. The texts we noted stress his obedience to his Father's will in taking the cup of suffering. However, this will of the Father is prompted by his loving desire to save the human family. Thus Jesus said, "It is the will of him who sent me that I should lose nothing of what he has given me; rather I should raise it up on the last day." (6:39; also, 17:12) Before the final supper, the evangelist notes that Jesus loved his disciples "to the end" (13:1). This may simply mean to the fullest extent, but it is hard to exclude the meaning that it was until the final end or completion on the cross when Jesus said that it was finished (19:30). This motivation is confirmed in the sixth sign, the raising of Lazarus. When Jesus resolved to go to Lazarus in Judea, his disciples were alarmed because they knew the Master's life was in danger (11:8). However, Jesus decided to go, knowing this would mean his own death. Thus the writer brings out symbolically (the raising of Lazarus is the sign of the raising of Christians) that Jesus died out of love in order to make others live. For this reason, the author stressed that Jesus loved Lazarus, Martha and Mary (11:5).

Jesus' mother at the cross is the most important witness of this motivating love. When Jesus gave her to the beloved disciple and his community, she became also a remembering mother and bearer of the tradition of Jesus' motivation of love. She well understood that the complete meaning of

Jesus' death was found in this loving gift of himself for his disciples. Since the mother is also in a successor role in her connection with the disciple, his own mother's care and concern for the disciples would be the same as that of Jesus. Thus Mary's role as a mother is a double one. First of all, she is a most important bearer of the tradition of the reality of Jesus' death, how he died, and in a connected manner, who he really was. Secondly, she embodies this tradition in a living way by her maternal continuation of Jesus' love for his disciples. How she does both of these in the full life of the community will be partly illustrated in the first sign at Cana.

JESUS' MOTHER IN THE FIRST SIGN, CANA OF GALILEE (2:1-12)

Because of the chiastic arrangement, we would expect the first and last signs to have a very close relationship: the first is included in the last, and the last completes the first. On the surface, there are common elements in both: Jesus' mother, the "hour," the thirst or lack of wine, the obedience motif, the wine/blood/water. The Cana story opens with the mother of Jesus present at a wedding, and with Jesus and his disciples also invited. Of course, a wedding feast is a well-known symbol of the messianic days (Isa. 54:4-8; 62:4-5). The wedding and the banquet are symbols used elsewhere by Jesus (Matt. 8:11; 9:15; 22:1-14). Abundant wine is the main ingredient of such festivities. To run short on such an occasion would be a long remembered public embarrassment for any married couple.

On her own initiative, or at the behest of the guests or family, Mary brings up the matter to Jesus and says, "They have no wine." Jesus responds (literally), "What is it to me and to you, woman? My hour has not yet come" (2:4). This statement seems to have a negative nuance. However, C.H. Giblin[47] has pointed out through Johannine parallels that

---

[47]pp. 197-211. This format is found in 2:1-11; 4:46-54; 7:2-14; 11:1-44.

the words do not necessarily mean a refusal to act. They imply that if Jesus acts it will be in accord with *his* own conscious purpose and design, not that of others. Therefore, at Cana he will not act according to the expectations of Mary or the people, but in line with his *hour*, a time that will show his true relationship with the Father and with his people. What Jesus wants to accomplish at Cana will only be shown through the seventh and last sign on the cross. This may mean that the initial wonder-work or miracle requested by Mary/the people, is not in Jesus' design. This seems to parallel the interconnected fourth sign of the loaves. There the people misinterpret the sign and understand it in the sense that Jesus will be another Moses and wonder-worker, bringing miraclulous bread like that provided by Moses in the desert. Jesus refused to go along with this, and hid from them, fearing the crowd would try to make him a king (6:14). In the situation of the Johannine community, this might refer to Jewish Christians whose views of Jesus were limited to that of a Messiah and sign worker.[48] If the purpose of Jesus' mother in the narrative reflects this, then Jesus refuses to act with this motive, but only in view of this approaching hour on the cross, and the meaning of the seventh sign. Other symbolic elements may be present,[49] but we wish to deal primarily with what Mary actually does in the text.

After the transition point of meaning in regard to Jesus' hour (2:4; cf. also 19:27), Jesus' mother tells the waiters, "Do whatever he tells you" (2:5). Jesus' mother now acts toward the waiters (and community) in accord with the maternal

---

[48]R.E. Brown describes one of the groups in the Johannine Community in this manner, but does not connect them with this text. *Community of the Beloved Disciple*, pp. 169.

[49]Other accessory areas of symbolism such as Mary as a representative image of the church, or as the new Eve have been suggested both in the Cana story and at the foot of the cross. Descriptions and basis for these are given by R.E. Brown, *The Gospel According to John*, vol. 1, pp. 107-109; vol. 2, pp. 923-927. However, since we suggest in this study that Mary's primary role is that of a maternal rememberer and bearer of tradition, we will not enter into discussion about accessory symbolism.

remembering role emphasized in the seventh sign. The emphasis is on perfect obedience to Jesus' word. This is noted three times: by Mary's word, by the waiters filling the jars as Jesus directed, and by their obedience to his command to bring the jars to the chief steward. We note the parallel to the seventh sign, where Jesus obeys the scriptures and God's plan by taking the imperfect bitter wine as the cup of suffering prepared by his Father (19:28-30). Thus Mary directs the community to obey Jesus' words, just as he has obeyed his Father's.

The episode at Cana may then mean that the choice wine of the new age can only be prepared in obedience to Jesus' words, just as the parallel blood/water/spirit from Jesus' side was only made possible by his acceptance of the imperfect, bitter "blood of the grape" in obedience to his Father. The community must participate in Jesus' hour and its meaning if they wish to receive the choice wine and Spirit made possible by his death. Jesus' mother has witnessed this death and acts in her remembering role by pointing to imitation and duplication of her son's obedience.

In addition, we noted in the seventh sign that Jesus' mother also became a true mother of the beloved disciple/ community by her understanding of the meaning of Jesus' death in terms of his love for those entrusted to him by the Father. We observed that Jesus' gift of his mother to the community included a transfer of this love in the person who most appreciated what his death stood for. Is this aspect also found at Cana? If the sign is interpreted in accord with Jesus' final hour, there are some indications that this is present also. Jesus' mother does take the initiative to present he community's need of wine to her son. Trusting an answer to her request, Mary gives directions to the waiters. This seems to indicate that she is an important person at the banquet. The role of responsibility for hospitality, food and wine usually fell upon a mother, and here she seems to act according to that model.

In what way could Mary's continuing role within the community be explained? One way could be through her symbolic identity with the church.[50] At Cana, she could represent the church as a concerned mother asking for the new wine of the spirit and presenting obedience to Jesus' word understood in light of his death as a means to obtain it. A second possible way is that of Mary as a heavenly intercessor. This is not found in the fourth gospel by any kind of direct evidence. However, it would fit in and be in no way contradictory to it as well as supported by acceptable biblical models. There can be nothing, of course, similar to Jesus' continual prayer for his disciples and for all believers, a prayer that goes far beyond his earthly life (chap. 17). Mary cannot be placed in this category with Jesus, and yet she cannot be separated from him either.

However, in connection with Jesus' prayer and Mary's permanent association with him in his hour, we can look to some biblical models outside the fourth gospel that indicate the importance of accessory mediator roles. These do not indicate proof that Mary was considered in such a role, but at least show that it would by no means be considered unlikely. The second book of Maccabees records the belief that the dead Onias, a former high priest, "prayed with outstretched hands for the whole Jewish community," and that the ancient Jeremiah, prompted by love of his brothers, fervently prayed for the people and their city (15:11-16). In the N.T. book of Revelation, the 24 presbyters around the throne of God have special bowls of incense which are described as the "prayers of God's holy people" (5:8). While their identity is uncertain—they may be a heavenly council of angelic beings or the saints of the OT and NT—they present the prayers of the faithful to God. In addition, this function of offering the faithful's prayers to God is also found in 8:3, where an angel comes and stands before the altar with a golden censer with much incense to mingle with the prayers of all the people. Similar to these models, perhaps the Johannine community considered Mary as continuing her function as a loving mother by offering their

---

[50]Cf. note 49.

petitions to her son. If so, the petition of Jesus' mother at Cana, and her initiative would hint at this function.

Summary: A chiastic structure for the seven signs in John, with the seventh sign at the cross in 19:25-37 offers a more complete source for appraising Jesus' mother's role at Cana and in the gospel. In this model, first and seventh sign complete one another, with the fourth sign of the loaves at the center of the chiasm and of the gospel. Mary's part and witness in these signs are a key to her role as mother, as well as to understanding the beloved disciple as a legitimate successor to Jesus and model for the believer as well as the community. As a remembering mother and carrier of tradition, Jesus' mother is the preeminent witness of who Jesus is, how Jesus died, and the effects of his death. The first and seventh signs carry the common elements of the presence of Jesus' mother, the centrality of the "hour," the obedience focus, as well as the interconnection of water/ wine/ Spirit.

Their meaning sheds light on the central fourth sign of the loaves to which both first and seventh point. The first sign at Cana appears to bring Mary's role into the community's life and worship, in view of the meaning of Jesus' hour. Jesus' mother directs them to obey Jesus as he obeyed his Father on the cross. Thus a new wine, prepared under obedience to Jesus and in the same spirit as the cross can become a reality.

7

The Apocalypse:
The Mysterious Woman
Clothed with the Sun
(12:1-17)

The book of Revelation (Apocalypse is the Greek title) has a distinct literary form from all the books studied so far. This will have a great bearing on its interpretation, especially in regard to Mary. This literary form is called "apocalyptic," from the Greek word *apokalyptō*, meaning to "remove a veil from." This veil refers to a hidden divine plan behind human history. In the book of Revelation, only this divine plan can give hope during a time of intense Roman governmental pressure on Christians toward the end of the first century A.D. At this time, believers felt they were fighting an apparently losing battle against powerful Roman authority, relentlessly pushing them to conformity even to the extent of joining emperor worship and participating in state religious rituals. Severe punishment, even death, could be the result of disobedience. To rescue them from this desperate situation, Christians could only look forward to a coming judgment of God and the return of Jesus. But when would all this happen?

Apocalyptic literature centers about the certainty and time of this great event. This is known only by God, yet he can and does reveal his secret plans to chosen ones. In this book, he does so to a certain John (not necessarily the John in the gospel) who has been exiled by Roman authority to the island of Patmos (off the western coast of modern Turkey) because of his steadfast witness to Jesus (1:9). John receives a vision of the risen Jesus in which this secret divine plan is revealed for the sake of the faithful. However, the revelation language is typical dream or visionary language using images and symbols taken not only from the bible but other contemporary literature. Adding to the difficulty, the vision often conveys its message through discoveries of secret or hidden meanings in many O.T. Scriptures that are no longer as familiar to us as they were to the early church. Also, the sense of time in apocalyptic literature is different from our own. Past, present and future are not distinct. This is because future is already present for God, but for us it is yet to come. This is why God is described as the one "who is and who was and who is to come" (1:4) or the "first and the last" (1:17).

The above difficulties regarding apocalyptic literature have led to a great variety of scholars' interpretations on the Apocalypse. In reference to our text, many interpreters[51] have found no place for Mary; others equally numerous have stated that a description of Jesus' mother is primary; still others take a middle viewpoint giving Mary a secondary place in the text. For reader convenience the significant verses are below.

> And a great portent appeared in heaven, a woman clothed with the sun, with the moon under her feet, and on her head a crown of twelve stars; she was with child and she cried out in her pangs of birth, in anguish for delivery. And another portent appeared in heaven; behold, a great red dragon, with seven heads and ten horns, and seven diadems upon his heads. His tail swept down a third of the stars of heaven, and cast them to the earth. And the

[51]A convenient summary of both sides may be found in *Mary in the New Testament*, pp. 235-239.

dragon stood before the woman who was about to bear a child, that he might devour her child when she brought it forth; she brought forth a male child, one who is to rule the nations with a rod of iron, but her child was caught up to God and to his throne, and the woman fled into the wilderness, where she has a place prepared by God, in which to be nourished for one thousand two hundred and sixty days (Apoc. 12:1-6).

And when the dragon saw that he had been thrown down to the earth, he pursued the woman who had borne the male child. But the woman was given the two wings of the great eagle that she might fly from the serpent into the wilderness, to the place where she is to be nourished for a time, and times, and half a time. The serpent poured water like a river out of his mouth after the woman, to sweep her away with the flood. But the earth came to the help of the woman, and the earth opened its mouth and swallowed the river which the dragon had poured from his mouth. Then the dragon was angry with the woman, and went off to make war on the rest of her offspring, on those who keep the commandments of God and bear testimony to Jesus. And he stood on the sand of the sea. (Apoc. 12:13-17).

In our interpretation, we will follow most modern scholars in seeing the mother and child as representing first God's people beginning with Israel and continuing (in Christian belief) with the church. This people of God, as bearers of the messianic hope, is symbolized by a mother giving birth to a child who will be a ruler and king. However, secondarily and inseparably included in the first is Mary as mother of the Messiah. Since the text was written by a first century Christian for a Christian audience, Mary could not be excluded from that sense by an audience that knows her to be the mother of Jesus.

The preceding chapters in the Apocalypse must be kept in mind to situate the text and its meaning. In chapter five, God held in his hand a mysterious sealed scroll, representing his secret plan for the world. No one is able to open and reveal this plan except Jesus, the slain Lamb (5:2-14). The Lamb opens the seals one by one. A terrifying picture follows of every kind of evil in world history: war, famine, pestilence, earthquakes and the apparent triumph of evil powers over the just. Yet all these are subject to divine control and are a test for the faithful whom God preserves from harm. Despite the overwhelming crescendo of evil, God announces good news to the world symbolized by the little scroll in chap. 10:1-7, which begins the central section (10-15) of the Apocalypse.[52] This good news is brought to people by the prophets, some of whom are even killed by their enemies, but death does not conquer them (11:3-13).

Chapter 12 and the sign of the Woman comes at a great turning point in the Apocalypse. The seventh angel blows his seventh trumpet and announces the final phase of the kingdom of God and ultimate victory (12:15-18). God is about to reveal himself completely. God's Temple in heaven is opened and the Holy Ark of God is seen (11:19). What follows in the Woman's sign is a revelation of God's great plan in history to win a victory over evil through the woman and her offspring. Some of the more significant verses will illustrate this.

"A great portent (sign) appeared in heaven, a woman clothed with the sun, with the moon under her feet, and on her head a crown of twelve stars" (12:1). A sign in the bible is typically God's proof for his designs as shown to human beings. The sign is "in the heaven" because it takes place in the divine realm first of all. The sun, moon and stars are descriptive elements of "heaven" or sky from which, in the ancient view, the stars hung like chandeliers, and across which the sun and moon ran their course. The sun, moon and stars belong to God and manifest him (Psalm 8). So the woman's clothing with the sun seems to indicate God's special presence and working in her. This comes out in direct

---

[52]E. Fiorenza's study of the literary structure of the Apocalypse argues that this section lies at the document's center.

contrast to the dragon who bears a divine resemblance with his seven heads, like the seven spirits of God (4:5-6). The stars in Apocalypse are a symbol of God's light-giving presence in his people through guardian spirits (1:20). In Joseph's O.T. dream, the sun, moon and eleven stars represent all the family of Israel (Gen. 37:9).

"And she was with child and she cried out in her pangs of birth, in anguish for delivery (12:2)... she brought forth a male child, one who is to rule all the nations with a rod of iron (12:5)." The woman and child together are the sign; the messianic hope is involved because of the reference (from Psalm 2:9) of a child who is to rule all the nations with an iron rod. The dragon is hoping to destroy the child, but is not able to do so because of God's special protection (12:4-6). Adela Collins[53] has pointed out that the conflict between woman/offspring and dragon with a promise of the woman's victory seems to go back to the beginning of creation where God said to the serpent,

> "I will put enmity between you and the woman, and between your seed and her seed; he shall bruise your head and you shall bruise his heel (Gen. 3:15).

The head wound in the text indicates victory, in contrast to a heel injury. The author must have had the Genesis text in mind since he calls the dragon "the ancient serpent, who is called the devil and Satan, the deceiver of the whole world" (12:9).

The woman/child symbol of hope continues in other O.T. important texts. Among these are the following: the promised offspring to Abraham and Sarah (Gen. 12:1-2; 15:4; 17:19-21; 18:9-15); the promises made to David about the continuity of the dynasty through future sons (2 Sam. 7:12-16) and references to Psalm 2 in Apoc. 2:27; 12:5; the woman bringing forth a future child and son are also in Isaiah 7:14; 9:6-7. At times the whole people of Israel is likened to a

---

[53]pp. 86-87.

mother bringing forth unexpected children because of God's presence in his people (Isa. 54:1-2).

Where does Mary appear in this text, if she does appear at all? We have seen that the text has a much broader scope than the birth of Jesus from Mary at Bethlehem. The text envisions God's plan in all history with the image of mother/child bringing out his continuing care for Israel in promising her a future child, king and Messiah. Mary and her son Jesus are central to this design but only a part of it. The workings of God's plan precede Jesus' birth and continue to work after it, for the woman has other offspring (12:17), perhaps the church, against which the dragon will battle. Thus the mother/child image in Apoc. 12 transcends the birth of Jesus and takes in all of history. It is God's chosen sign of victory over the powers of evil represented by the dragon and his later "incarnation" in the beast, symbolic of absolute secular power.

We may conclude that Mary is the woman in Apoc. 12 in an inclusive way as part of a larger and timeless mother/child sign. It would be hard to think of a first century Christian author as excluding Mary and her child from this image. Yet the text does not give us any personal information about Jesus' mother. Is there anything new at all in this text? In comparison with Matthew's image of mother-child in the divine plan, some new elements may be seen: 1) A broader, more universal perspective in God's creative work in every mother bearing a child, expecially those leading to the birth of the messianic offspring of the people Israel; 2) the woman/child in Apoc. 12 is in a conflict situation with the dragon and his allies. Their victory is a sign of victory and hope for all future believers and offspring of the woman who continue the struggle against evil powers led by the dragon; 3) The victory comes only through a very painful and long struggle. This is illustrated through the childbirth pangs which may signify the traditional messianic woes of the last times. The struggle also appears in the image of the dragon waiting to devour the newborn child and continually pursuing the woman, who would certainly have been

captured by the dragon were it not for the repeated intervention of God (12:4-6; 13-15).

THE UNITY AND DIVERSITY OF NEW TESTAMENT
PORTRAITS OF MARY

We have seen the great diversity within the N.T. regarding
Jesus' mother: the near silence of Pauline letters, the almost
hostile picture in Mark and the prominence of Mary found
in John and Luke. This diversity, however, gradually
disappeared as the New Testament became considered as a
unified body of writings. Thus, the more prominent Marian
texts in Luke and John became the normative sources for a
portrait of Jesus' mother.

This unifying movement began with the gospels which
gradually became considered as a "fourfold unity." Justin
Martyr simply refers to "the gospels" around the middle of
the second century although we are not certain he was
familiar with all four. Around 170, Tatian prepared a
harmony of the four gospels called the *Diatessaron* which
became very popular, especially in Syria. Toward the end of
the second century, Clement of Alexandria refers to the
"four gospels that have been handed down to us" (Strom.
III. 93.1). Irenaeus later calls the gospels "a fourfold shape
held together by one spirit" (Her. III, 11.8).

The letters of Paul, really the first Christian literature,
acquired a second place added to the four gospels and after
them. Among the gospels, Mark was least quoted and used
because of its "incomplete" nature. Thus as time went on, the
earlier diversity between Christian communities gradually
disappeared along with the remembrance that the literature
was originally addressed to separated local communities.
This meant that the "more complete" image of Mary found
in John and Luke became normative as the collected and
canonical New Testament gradually took shape and received
acceptance.

8

Mary in Second-Century Literature

For convenience, these texts can be divided into three
general groups: New Testament Apocrypha, Jewish Christian
Apocalypses and the Works of Christian Writers. The first
group, N.T. apocrypha, are books that were never placed on
the official church lists or canon of N.T. books. However
some of them had widespread popularity and great influence
in the early church, especially in regard to Mary. Some may
have preserved independent traditions not found in the four
gospels. This extra-gospel literature was held suspect by the
later church because it emanated from Christian groups
considered to be heretical. For many centuries, Christian
authorities placed most of these works in lists of forbidden
reading for the ordinary people.

Despite this, some of this literature has had an important
impact in the development of Mariology and popular
Christian piety.

1. New Testament Apocrypha

We begin with the most influential book: the *Protoevangelium of James*, written under the pseudonym of
James the brother of Jesus, probably a short time after 150
A.D. This is the first Christian book written completely
about Mary. To assess its contribution, it will be helpful to
outline its contents.

The story begins with Mary's parents Joachim and Anna independently praying for a child in their old age. The names seem taken from the O.T. Joachim is found in Susanna, verse 4, where he is described (as in the Proto E.) as very rich with an only daughter. Anna is prominent in 1 Sam. 1-2 as the mother of Samuel the prophet. The stories are similar: the birth of a child in response to prayer and the presentation of the child to the priest in the Temple. In addition, our author has drawn considerably from Luke's gospel where Mary's Magnificat is also influenced by Anna in 2 Samuel. Despite this, the names of Mary's parents were taken as fact by later Christianity and are honored as saints today. Anna, like Mary in Luke, is visited by an angel and promised a child. In response, Anna vows that the child will be "a gift to the Lord My God" (words of 1 Sam, 1:11, where Anna, mother of Samuel promises the same). Joachim independently is notified by an angel about the coming event. Anna, his wife, gives birth to Mary in her seventh month of pregnancy.

At the age of three, Mary's parents present Mary to the priests in the Temple so she can be a lifelong virgin, in the company of other Temple virgins. (There is no trace of any such custom in Judaism but the model seems to be Anna's presentation of Samuel to the Lord in 1 Sam. 2:22-28). When Mary reaches twelve, the Temple priests decide she must leave the Temple, probably because women's periods brought about a "contagious" time of religious "uncleanness" for seven days each month (cf. Lev. 15:19-24). The priests search for an aged widower to be Mary's guardian, and Joseph is chosen by a special sign from God. Here we find for the first time the idea that Joseph had children from a former marriage.

The annunciation to Mary at age 16 is described with liberal quotations from Luke and added details. Joseph is shocked in discovering her pregnancy, but "James" quotes the Gospel of Matthew where an angel advises him not to fear. However, the priests learn of the matter and subject the couple to the adultery test found in Numbers 5:11-31. Both are found innocent. As for the birth at Bethlehem, Mary laughs before delivery instead of experiencing birth pangs. A great light appears in a Bethlehem *cave* and the child suddenly appears with Mary virginally intact even in childbirth. This is even guaranteed by a midwife's physical examination! Other miraculous events follow, but the details above contain the significant items.

To assess this book, we should first ascertain whether it adds anything to the historical Mary who gave birth to Jesus about 150 years before. "James" uses Luke and Matthew as sources which he liberally quotes. The O.T., especially the first chapters of 1 Samuel, seems woven into the story. There is a proliferation of miracles, even about details, that casts doubt on the author's sources. It is possible that the book contains some genuine historical reminiscences not in the gospels like the mention of the cave at Bethlehem but these are not essential facts. To understand the author's viewpoint, he seems obsessed to prove Mary's perpetual virginity to the extent of introducing fantastic (and even crude) details. He may be intending to answer accusations and slurs about Jesus' birth. We have seen that this may already have been part of Matthew's purpose, and we will find it recurring in later Christian documents.

However, the book tells us a great deal about Mary in the second century, since the story enjoyed widespread popularity. "James" furnished Christians with a "personal story" of Mary that filled in what was lacking in the gospels. The names of Mary's parents and the story of her childhood, the details of Jesus' conception and birth gave people images they could relate to. The description of Mary as a virgin not only before Jesus' birth (as in Matthew and Luke) but during and after, was a step toward a later common Christian teaching that Mary was "semper virgo," always a virgin. However, the author went to extremes in his argument. Even Mary's betrothal and marriage to Joseph found in the gospels (Matt. 1:18, 24; Luke 1:27) are omitted. Joseph becomes only a protector of the virgin, a widower with children from a previous marriage. Mary is even denied the normal child-delivery experience. Thus the author, perhaps unwittingly, "desexes" Mary with his excessive emphasis on her virginity.

The Protoevangelium of James maintained its influence for centuries in ancient and medieval art, in liturgy and stained glass scenes in the great churches and cathedrals of Europe even to this day. Its popularity continued despite severe opposition from later Christian writers and authorities. St. Jerome's opposition led to its condemnation by Popes Damasus, Innocent I, and Gelasius. The sixteenth-century Protestant reformers came out strongly against it, even though Luther relates that St. Anne (from the same book) gave him his call as a monk!

THE GOSPEL TO THE HEBREWS

Only a few fragments quoted by early Christian writers have come down to us from this second-century work. One of them focuses attention on James, brother of Jesus, who receives a special apparition of the risen Lord. The following fragments speak of Mary:

> 1. It is written in the Gospel of the Hebrews: When Christ wished to come upon the earth to men, the good Father summoned a mighty power in heaven, which was called Michael, and entrusted Christ to the care thereof. And the power came into the world, and it was called Mary, and Christ was in her womb seven months.[54]
> 3. And if any accept the gospel of the Hebrews—here the Savior says: "Even so did my Mother, the Holy Spirit, take me by one of my hairs and carry me away on to the great mountain of Tabor."[55]

[54]These can be found in Hennecke, p. 163 whose translation and dating study we have utilized.

[55]Hennecke, Vol. 1, p. 164.

Both of these texts seem to be gnostic-influenced, with their omission of the human reality of Jesus' birth. In the first text, Mary is more an angelic power than a human mother. In the second, Jesus' mother is the Holy Spirit only.

THE GOSPEL OF THE NAZARAEANS

This is another fragmentary gospel of which sixteen parts are extant. Little is known about it except that it addresses a Jewish Christian audience. The following is the only text directly about Mary, although some medieval fragments describe Joseph and the Magi, whose actual names are given:

> 2. Behold the mother of the Lord and his brethren said to him: John the Baptist baptizes unto the remission of sins, let us go and be baptized by him. But he said to them: How have I sinned that I should go and be baptized by him? Unless what I have said is ignorance (a sin of ignorance).[56]

The text seems more concerned about Jesus' sinlessness as a doctrine than about his mother Mary.

THE GOSPEL OF THE EBIONITES

The Ebionites were Jewish Christians who discounted Jesus' humanity and thus omitted Jesus' birth from their documents. In one of the seven fragments of this gospel, great attention is given to Jesus' baptism as the source of his messiahship and divine origin. Fragment 5 has the following:

> Moreover, they deny that he was a man, evidently on the ground of the word which the Savior spoke when it was reported to him: "Behold, thy mother and thy brethren

[56]Hennecke, Vol. 1, pp. 146-147.

stand without," namely: Who is my mother and who are my brethren? And he stretched forth his hand towards his disciples and said: These are my brethren and mother and sisters, who do the will of the Father.[57]

This fragment, and those of other "gospels" previously quoted are important for us because they illustrate an excessive emphasis on Jesus' divinity to the exclusion of his humanity.

For this reason, perhaps, the *Protoevangelium of James* and other documents went to such extremes in contrast. The emphasis on Mary's virginity and motherhood served to bring together both human and divine elements in Jesus to counteract docetic and gnostic leanings.

THE LETTER OF THE APOSTLES

This letter contains a supposed dialogue between the risen Christ and the eleven disciples. During the dialogue, the risen Christ stresses his bodily reality against Cerinthus and Simon who have denied it. At the same time, Jesus teaches his absolute unity with the Father. Mary is as an important witness of Jesus' twofold nature:

> We believe that the *word*, which *became flesh* through the holy virgin Mary was carried (conceived) in her womb by the Holy Spirit, and was born not by the lust of the flesh but by the will of God and was wrapped (in swaddling clothes) and made known at Bethlehem; and that he was reared and grew up, as we saw. This is what our Lord Jesus Christ did, who was delivered by Joseph and Mary his mother to where he might learn letters.[58] (1:3-4)

Of special interest is the reference to John 1:13, "born not by the lust of the flesh," which describes Jesus' virginal birth,

[57] Hennecke, Vol. 1, p. 158.
[58] Hennecke, Vol. 1, p. 192-193.

not the birth of Christians as in most Greek manuscripts. This meaning accords with that of a number of versions[59] of John 1:15 that have the words in connection with Jesus' virginal birth.

There is also the following Marian information in 1:14 of the Letter of the Apostle:

> On that day, when I took the form of the angel Gabriel, I appeared to Mary and spoke with her. Her heart received me and she believed; I formed myself and entered into her womb; I became flesh.[60]

The text seems to try to unite belief in Jesus the eternal Word of God (as in John 1:1-13) with belief in his human origin from the virgin Mary.

ACTS OF THE APOSTLES

These were stories and travelogues of Peter, Paul and other apostles written to fill in gaps left by the gospels and Luke's Acts of the Apostles. The acts of Paul were written toward the end of the second century, since Tertullian who died around 220 A.D., refers to them. In a so-called letter of the Corinthians to Paul we find reference to Simon and Clobius who falsely teach:

> That there is no resurrection of the flesh, and that the creation of man is not God's (work), and that the Lord is not come in the flesh, nor was he born of Mary, and that the world is not of God but of the angels.[61] (1:12-15)

We notice here the typical gnostic teachings about dualism (in the evil origin of the world), denial of a future resurrection,

---

[59]These are principally versions of this verse as cited by a number of Church Fathers.

[60]Hennecke, Vol. 1, p. 199.

[61]Hennecke, Vol. 2, p. 374.

and the reality of Jesus' humanity. Paul counters this by writing back to them what he has received "through the apostles,"

> That our Lord Jesus Christ was born of Mary of the seed of David, when the Holy Spirit was sent from heaven by the Father into her, that he might come into this world and redeem all flesh through his own flesh. (3:5-6)[62]

Also, in further confirmation,

> God the almighty,... sent the (Holy) spirit (through fire) into Mary the Galilean, who believed with all her heart, and she received the Holy Spirit in her womb that Jesus might enter the world in order that the evil one might be conquered by the same flesh by which he held sway. (3:12-15)[63]

The Acts of Peter were written shortly before the Acts of Paul since the author quotes the latter. In Peter's story, the apostle has a debate with Simon the magician in the Roman forum. Simon asks the crowd if a God can be born or crucified, and Peter replies,

> The prophet says, "In the last times a boy is born of the Holy Spirit; his mother knows not a man, nor does anyone claim to be his father" and again he says, "she has given birth and has not given birth."... and again, "Behold a virgin shall conceive in the womb." And another prophet ..."We have neither heard her voice, nor has a midwife come in..." Another prophet says, "He was not born from the womb of a woman, but came down from a heavenly place."[64]

---

[62] Hennecke, Vol. 2, p. 375.
[63] Hennecke, Vol. 2, p. 376.
[64] Hennecke, Vol. 2, p. 307.

Thus we see in both the Acts of Peter and Paul that the tradition of Mary as virgin-mother is very important for answering gnostic-influenced questions and beliefs. There is also a personal note since Mary's own faith is considered essential.

2. Jewish Apocalyptic Writings With Christian Revisions

These writings were originally accounts of visions about God's future plans given to great Jewish leaders and prophets of the past. Christians made additions to these with specific references to the life of Jesus. The following is part of a vision from the *Ascension of Isaiah*:

> And he (Joseph) did not approach Mary, but kept her as a holy virgin, although she was with child,... and after two months, when Joseph was in his house, and his wife Mary, but both alone, it came to pass that Mary beheld with her eyes a small child and she was amazed. And when her amazement wore off, her womb was found as it was before she was with child. (11:5-9).... And I saw: in Nazareth he sucked the breast like a baby, as was customary, so he would not be recognized (11:17)[65]

This text is similar to the *Protoevangelium of James* in its description of the virginity of Mary and the sudden appearance of the child without normal delivery. Yet the child is definitely real and human.

The Sibylline Oracles were important to Jews and Christians alike because of the belief that God spoke of the future not only through Jewish prophets but also through Greek and Roman poets and oracles. The following is a Christian addition to one of these stories. Again we find the

---

[65] Hennecke, Vol. 2, p. 661.

image of the laughing virgin in this poetic paraphrase of Luke:

> First then the holy, mighty form of Gabriel was displayed and second, the archangel addressed the maiden in speech: "In thine immaculate bosom, virgin, do thou receive God."... and the maiden laughed, her cheeks flushed scarlet ... Then she took courage, The Word flew into her body, made flesh in time and brought to life in her womb, was moulded to mortal frame and became a boy by virgin birth pangs; this, a great wonder to mortals. (459-472)[66]

The following poetic verses are found at the end of Book I of the Sibylline Oracles, but their date is uncertain:

> When the maid shall give birth to the Logos of God most High,
> But as wedded wife shall give to the Logos a name,
> Then from the east shall a star shine forth in the midst of the day
> Radiant and gleaming down from heaven above,
> Proclaiming a great sign to Mortal Men
> Yes, then shall the Son of the great God come to men,
> Clothed in flesh, like unto mortals on earth.[67]

At this point we can briefly sum up our findings from second century N.T. Apocrypha and Jewish-Christian Apocalyptic writings. The *Protoevangelium of James,* especially, is a witness to popular interest in Mary as a person. From an apologetic viewpoint, the constant emphasis on Mary as "Virgin as well as Mother" was very important to counteract gnostic-influenced teachings that denied or discounted the reality of Jesus' humanity. The image of the

---

[66] Hennecke, Vol. 2, p. 740.
[67] Hennecke, Vol. 2, p. 709.

Virgin-Mother was a guarantee both of Jesus' real human nature and his ultimate divine origin.

3. Second-Century Christian Writers

IGNATIUS OF ANTIOCH

Ignatius of Antioch is one of the most important of early Christian writers due to his closeness to the age of the apostles and his important position in Antioch, the missionary center of the early church. We do not know his birthdate, but he seems to have been martyred in Rome between 98-117, the second half of Trajan's reign. He probably became a convert late in life, for he refers to himself as "born out of due time," (To the Romans, 9) like Paul (1 Cor. 15:8). The writings of Ignatius[68] are a collection of seven letters written shortly before his death to the churches of Ephesus, Magnesia, Tralles, Rome, Philadelphia, Smyrna, and to Polycarp, Bishop of Smyrna.

Ignatius' letters are a key witness of Christian beliefs in the early second century in a large city where there were traditions from both Peter and Paul (Gal. 2:11-14; Acts 15). Especially significant for us are the references to Mary, not just in passing but in connection with central Christian beliefs and in counteraction to errors about the nature of Jesus. These errors, as we shall point out, concerned the reality of the birth, death and resurrection body of Jesus. They were also linked to the reality of Jesus' presence in the Eucharist.

In Ignatius' letter to the Ephesians, we have the following Marian references: the first is in response to unworthy Christian teachers:

---

[68]References and translations of Ignatius are from the *Fathers of the Church*, Trans., G.G. Walsh.

> There is one Doctor active in both body and soul,
> begotten and yet unbegotten, God in Man, True life in
> death, son of Mary and Son of God, first able to suffer
> and then unable to suffer. (To the Ephesians 7).

Note the emphasis on Jesus' ability to suffer and die; both of
these appear in conjunction with "son of Mary" as a
confirmation of Jesus humanity.

> For our God Jesus Christ was, according to God's
> dispensation, the fruit of Mary's womb, of the seed of
> David; He was born and baptized in order that he might
> make the water holy by his passion. The maidenhood of
> Mary, and her childbearing and also the death of the Lord
> were hidden from the prince of the world—three re-
> sounding mysteries wrought in the silence of God. (To the
> Ephesians, 18-19)

Here, Jesus' human Davidic origin is made possible by
Mary's womb. The human birth, baptism and passion unite
to make the baptism of Christians effective. Mary's virginity,
childbearing and Jesus' death are placed on the same level as
three great mysteries hidden from the devil. It is significant
to see these named together for Christians as essential
mysteries of the faith. Mary is not an addition to the gospel
but intimately connected to its center.

After a warning to stay clear of heretics and close to the
bishop, Ignatius writes to the Trallians,

> Be deaf when anyone speaks to you apart from Jesus
> Christ, who was of the race of David, the son of Mary,
> who was truly born and ate and drank, who was truly
> persecuted under Pontius Pilate,and was really crucified
> and died. (89)

Again stress is laid on the reality of Jesus' birth, humanity,
suffering and death with Mary having an essential part and
witness. The application to docetic errors occurs in the

following verse, "If, as some say who are godless in the sense that they are without faith, 'he merely seemed to suffer'—it is they themselves who merely seemed to suffer.'" (10)

Writing to Smyrna, Ignatius places Jesus' birth to a Virgin in the middle of a credal formula:

> He (Jesus) was born of the Virgin and baptized by John...; that in his body, he was truly nailed to the cross for our sake under Pontius Pilate and Herod the Tetrarch,... so that through his resurrection, he might raise, for all ages, in the one body of his church a standard for the saints and faithful.... (1)

Once more this credal statement counteracts docetic or gnostic tendencies. In the next verse it is stated that Jesus truly suffered and truly rose: "he did not suffer merely in appearance, as some of the unbelievers say" (2). Following this, Peter is brought in as a witness that Jesus was actually felt and touched as a real body after his resurrection.

This human reality of Jesus' death and resurrection appears connected with the Eucharist. Referring to false teachers, Ignatius writes:

> They abstain from the Eucharist and from prayer because they do not admit that the Eucharist is the flesh of our Savior Jesus Christ, the flesh which suffered for our sins and which the Father ... raised from the dead. (To the Smyrnaeans, 6)

JUSTIN MARTYR

Here we find a valuable follow up to Luke and John, where we already noted the close connection between the Eucharist and Mary, St. Justin Martyr.[69]

Like Ignatius, Justin is called an Apostolic Father because

---

[69]References and translations of Justin are from *Fathers of the Church*, Trans. T.B. Falls.

he was so near the time of the Apostles. He was born in Samaria of Greco-Roman ancestry around the beginning of the second century. He received a thorough training in Greek and Roman philosophy before becoming a Christian convert. His works are especially valuable as the first systematic attempt to use philosophy as well as scripture in the defense of the Christian faith. He died as a martyr around 165 A.D. The first work in which Mary is named is the *Apologia I*, which Justin wrote "150 years after the birth of Christ" (1 Apol. 46). This work was addressed to the Imperial Roman government as an apologia for the Truth of Christianity. The second work, the *Dialogue with Trypho*, is a Christian defense against Judaism written some years later.

In both documents, Justin refers to the virgin birth of Jesus and to Mary his mother. First of all, this birth is in fulfillment of Isaiah 7:14 and the text "a virgin shall conceive." Justin refers to Isaiah despite his knowledge that the Hebrew text has "young woman," not "virgin" and that the text has been understood to refer to an immediate successor of Achaz, the king to whom it is addressed. Justin maintains the virginal origin of Jesus in opposition to Celsus who claims Jesus to be of mere human origin. In this same chapter, Justin shows his familiarity with Greek myths and stories about the gods impregnating virgins (Trypho 67). In another place, Justin distinguishes God's action in Mary from these stories because no sexual desires or intercourse had a part in Mary's event (I Apologia, 33). Justin actually appeals to the virginal conception as a proof that the child is truly "the first-born Word of God," "and at the same time man." This is because he (the Son) "became man by a virgin." Following this, Justin affirms that Jesus suffered contempt and pain to prove this humanity (I Apol. 63). This becomes more explicit in Trypho 100, where Justin states that "the first begotten of God,... became incarnate by a virgin of their race, and condescended to become a man without comeliness or honor, and subject to suffering." Even the title "Son of Man" in this chapter is traced to the virgin birth into the family of Abraham or Adam.

Most significant is the first statement in Christian literature about the parallel/contrast between Mary and Eve:

> He is born of the Virgin, in order that the disobedience caused by the serpent might be destroyed in the same manner in which it had originated. For Eve, an undefiled virgin, conceived the word of the serpent, and brought forth disobedience and death but the Virgin Mary, filled with faith and joy ... answered, "Be it done unto me according to thy word." And indeed she gave birth to him ... by whom God destroys both the serpent and those angels and men who have become like the serpent. (Trypho, 100)

The passage also marks the beginning of theological reflection about Mary as a person; for it is her obedience that makes possible the economy of salvation, with its victory over the serpent (the devil).

IRENAEUS, BISHOP OF LYON

Irenaeus is a third important bridge to apostolic times, though belonging more to a third generation of Christian teachers. The only key to his birthdate is his note (III, 3, 4 Massuet edition) that he knew Polycarp of Smyrna as a boy which indicates around 120-140 A.D. Irenaeus became bishop of Lyons, France about 177 and died around 202. His greatest work known only in Latin translation was *Adversus Haereses*. Irenaeus' works are especially valuable in giving us a detailed picture of the great variety in Christian teachings at that time. These are considered heresies by the author who counters them with arguments from the scripture, the apostolic tradition and the gospels. Irenaeus makes dozens of references to the Virgin Mary in his writing as an essential factor in his arguments.

What was Irenaeus so concerned about? He is very explicit, furnishing names of heretical teachers such as Cerinthus, Valentinus, Marcion, Simon and others as well as details about their teachings.

Of special concern to us are the following examples: that Christ, Son of God did not really assume human flesh (nor did he really die) on the cross. The Spirit of Christ came upon him at baptism and left before his death (I, 7, 2); the Son of God only clothed himself in human flesh for our benefit (I, 15, 2); Jesus did not really suffer but Simon of Cyrene was crucified instead (I, 23, 4); that Jesus was a real son of Joseph and Mary, but the Spirit of Christ came on him in the form of a dove and then departed before his death (I, 26, 1). All the above are typical docetic or gnostic views. To counter these, Irenaeus cites Mary and the virgin birth again and again as a first line of defense. To stress the reality of Jesus' human nature, the following are examples:

Irenaeus affirms that the eternal Word became human flesh, a son of men through Mary,

> He, therefore, the Son of God, our Lord, being the Word of the Father and the Son of man, since he had a generation as to his human nature from Mary—who was descended from mankind, and who was herself a human being—was made the son of Man (III, 19, 3).

The bishop of Lyons likes to call this the *sign of the Virgin* or the *sign of the Virgin/Emmanuel* fulfilling the prophecy of Isaiah 7:14, "A virgin shall conceive and bear a son." (III, 20, 3; 21, 4; also in *Proof of the Apostolic Preaching*, 54, 59). As with Ignatius and Justin before him, Irenaeus considers the virgin birth so important that he makes it part of a credal statement along with the central truths of the Christian faith. Irenaeus writes of those who "preserving the ancient tradition, believing in one God, the creator of heaven and earth,... by means of Christ Jesus, the Son of God, who,... condescended to be born of the virgin,... and having suffered under Pontius Pilate, and rising again, and having been received up in splendor, shall come in glory ..." (111, 4, 2).

Like Justin before him, Irenaeus also focuses attention on the person of Mary in developing the Eve-Mary contrast.

Mary is an obedient virgin, unlike Eve the virgin before her fall. Mary's obedience becomes, "the cause of salvation, both to herself and the whole human race: Mary was believing, Eve unbelieving" (III, 22, 1-4). It is noteworthy that Mary is considered to play a key role in the whole economy of salvation.

SECOND-CENTURY SUMMARY

First of all, Christological concerns influence the growth of Mary's prominence. Docetic and Gnostic views of the unreality of Jesus' humanity, suffering and death had to be countered. An emphasis on Mary's virginity in Jesus' conception and birth became a key argument against those tendencies. The virgin birth could preserve and put together Jesus' divinity and humanity. This virgin birth becomes so important that it is placed side by side with the death and resurrection of Jesus, the principal mysteries of the Christian faith. Thus we see a step toward the inseparable association of Mother and Child in the Christian church.

Secondly, interest in the person of Mary becomes very evident, especially with the popularity and influence of the *Protoevangelium of James.* There is also a growing sense of the importance of her life and virtues, especially her obedience and faith, on the whole economy of salvation ending with the statement of Irenaeus that Mary's obedience was "the cause of salvation, both to herself and the whole human race." In addition, the connections between Mary and the reality of Jesus' body in the Eucharist that we found in Luke and John continue to be made.

However, it should be noted that a number of prominent writers such as Clement of Rome and the author of the Shepherd of Hermes do not mention Mary at all. One factor is that the use of all of the four gospels only comes about gradually, with John as the latest (and strongest in Mary's connections with the cross). Only Irenaeus, at the close of the second century quotes all four liberally.

9

The Road to Ephesus and Mary's Triumph: 200-431, Part I

APOCRYPHAL LITERATURE

Infancy accounts, modeled on James' earlier work, continue their popularity, but little significant additional information is found about Mary. Among these are the Infancy story of Thomas, containing fantastic (and sometimes shocking) miracles performed by the child Jesus.

Interesting information is found in the Apocalypse of Paul, written toward the end of the fourth century. These contain Paul's revelations when he was lifted up in ecstasy to heaven (2 Cor. 12). There, the "Virgin Mary, the Mother of the Lord" receives Paul into heaven (46). She is accompanied by 200 angels singing hymns before her. Thus the text accords her the highest place in heaven and prepare the way for the later title "Queen of Heaven."[70]

The connection between the reality of the Eucharist and the Virgin Mary is also emphasized in this work: there are people sealed into the well of the abyss who are identified as:

> Those who have not confessed that Christ came in the flesh and that the Virgin Mary bore him, and who say

[70] Hennecke, Vol. 2, p. 790.

that the bread of the Eucharist and the cup of blessing are not the body and blood of Christ. (41)[71]

The so-called "Acts of Pilate" date probably from the fourth century. We find again the charge that Jesus' birth was illegitimate, a child of fornication. Pilate hears these charges brought by Jewish elders. However, twelve witnesses, whose names are given, come forward and swear that they were present at the betrothal of Mary and Joseph. (II, 4-5)[72]

The Gospel of Bartholomew contains a series of revelations given to this apostle by Jesus. Its date is uncertain, but it may contain materials from the third and fourth centuries. In these visions we find an image of Mary as intercessor that we have not yet encountered after the N.T. The apostles ask her to lead them in prayer. She does so, lifting her arms to heaven. In the prayer she calls upon the eternal Logos who was contained within her, but without pain. (II, 1-14)[73] She also states that her annunciation took place in the Temple (where she was fed by angels!) three years before the event (II, 15-21). In the document, Bartholomew and Peter address Mary as the tabernacle (tent) of the Most High (II, 4; IV, 4). This means she is like the Temple itself, the place of God's presence.

Once again, in Bartholomew, we find the Eve/Mary contrasts, but with a new twist: at creation God placed two great lights in heaven, the sun shining on Adam, and the moon on Eve. The moon became darkened and clouded because of Eve's sin, but in Mary's words, "In, me the Lord took up his abode, that I might restore the dignity of women" (IV, 5). Peter said to Mary: "You made good the transgression of Eve, changing her shame to joy" (IV, 6).

An unusual feature of this "gospel" is the appearance of a great cosmic mother image identified with Jesus' mother: Bartholomew exclaims,

---

[71] Hennecke, Vol. 2, p. 786.

[72] Hennecke, Vol. 1, p. 453.

[73] Hennecke, Vol. 1, p. 493.

O womb more spacious than a city! O womb wider than the span of heaven! O womb containing him whom the seven heavens do not contain. You contained him without pain and held in your bosom him who changed his being into the smallest of things. O womb that bore, concealed in your body, the Christ who has been made visible to Mary. O womb that became more spacious than the whole creation (III, 17-18; cf. 60-61 for similar expressions applied to Mary)[74]

This image of Mary as the great cosmic mother may have been an important element in the Christian encounter with the cult of the mother goddess in Europe and Asia Minor. In later times, the connection will become more explicit as churches dedicated to Mary are built over and replace holy places where the mother goddess cult once took place.

THE GOSPEL OF PHILIP[75]

This gnostic gospel was found in the collection of gnostic and gnostic-related Coptic documents found in Nag Hammadi, Egypt in the 1940's. Its approximate date is the second half of the third century. While other N.H. materials mention Mary, this is the most significant because of the clear gnostic view of Mary. The gospel of Philip does respect Mary. It numbers her among the three who always walked with the Lord: Mary his mother, her sister and the Magdalene (II, 3:63).

However, we find here a gnostic view of the virgin birth. This "virgin" is the Spirit, which is, in Elaine Pagel's explanation, "Mother and Virgin, the counterpart-and consort-of the Heavenly Father."[76] Consequently, Philip ridicules those who take a literal view of Mary's virginal birth:

[74]Hennecke, Vol. 1, p. 496-497.

[75]Found in Robinson, The Nag Hammadi Library, p. 131-151.

[76]p. 63.

> Some said, "Mary conceived by the Holy Spirit." They are
> in error. They do not know what they are saying. When
> did a woman ever conceive by a woman?[77]

This gnostic view of the "virgin birth" is valuable in ex-
plaining why orthodox Christianity took such pains in
emphasizing the literal nature of this event in order to
confirm the humanity of Christ.

By way of summary, apocryphal writings of this period
reveal the following significant elements: Mary is pictured as
a heavenly intercessor because of her first place in the
heavens. Belief in the virgin birth and the reality of the
Eucharist are connected. The charge of Jesus' illegitimacy is
refuted through the virgin birth. Mary repairs the fall of Eve
and raises the condition of women. She becomes identified
with the image of a great cosmic mother.

WESTERN WRITERS 200-431

During this period, Marian references become so frequent
that only excerpts from the most significant can be given
here.

HIPPOLYTUS OF ROME (c. 170-c. 235)

There is much confusion about his identity and life. He
was probably a Roman priest and counter-pope who wrote
very extensively in Greek. St. Hippolytus is a witness of an
ancient Christian creed, in which a baptismal question
concerns the virgin birth; "Do you believe in Christ Jesus,
the Son of God, who was born by the Holy Spirit from the
Virgin Mary".... (The Apostolic Trad. of St. Hippolytus
XXI, 12, 15).[78] These words are the same as those in the

---

[77]Robinson, p. 134.

[78]Palmer, p. 4.

"Apostles Creed" reported by Rufinus[79] (around 400) as going back to apostolic times. Hippolytus also has a passage relating indirectly to Mary's holiness, a subject that will later receive great attention. A fragment of a commentary on Ps. 22 (believed to be from Hippolytus) treats of the incorruptible wood of the Ark of the Covenant (Ex. 25:10). Our author writes, "The Lord was sinless, because in his humanity, he was fashioned out of incorruptible wood, that is to say, out of the Virgin and the Holy Spirit, lined within and without as with the purest gold of the Word of God."[80]

TERTULLIAN c. 160-after 220)[81]

Tertullian, a son of a Roman centurion, was probably born at Carthage, where he received a thorough education and engaged in law practice before becoming a Christian around 195, after what he calls a licentious youth. In reaction to his past, he became a rigorous ascetic and joined the extreme Montanists. Despite this, he was a gifted and learned writer of great renown in the west.

Tertullian adheres firmly to the virgin birth as part of a "rule of faith," one that is common to the apostolic churches. *(De praescriptione haereticorum,* cap. 13 and 20). Yet he does not consider virginity during and after birth as part of this (De carne Christi, cap. 23). He believes that Mary had other physical sons and daughters by normal marriage after the virgin birth (Adv. Marcionem, lib. 3, cap 11). Tertullian's statement is quite extraordinary considering his extreme ascetic views in other places. His view that Mary was a virgin only before Jesus' birth would later trigger a severe condemnation by Jerome.

Tertullian also develops the Mary/Eve parallelism, em-

---

[79]Palmer, p. 4.

[80]Palmer, p. 15.

[81]Most of references to Tertullian, Cyprian, Hilary of Poitiers, Ambrose, Zeno, Jerome and Augustine that follow are from W.J. Burghardt, "Mary in Western Patristic Thought" in J.B. Carol, ed., *Mariology*, Vol. 1.

phasizing Mary's obedience, faith, virginity and victory over Satan (De carne Christi, cap. 17). Even though in later life he became a Montanist, with their gnostic tendencies, he still remained convinced of the importance and reality of Jesus' human birth through Mary. He writes, "his (Jesus') flesh, though not born of seed, still proceeded from the flesh" (De carne Christi, cap. 21).

CYPRIAN OF CARTHAGE (d. 258).

While his birthdate is not known, Cyprian became a Christian about 236 after receiving a thorough education. He became bishop of Carthage, where he was a courageous leader of his flock despite severe persecution and finally martyrdom.

Cyprian continues the line of witnesses connecting Mary to the prophecy of Isaiah 7:14, and Gen. 3:14-15. The fulfillment of Isaiah is a sign of the birth of one who is "man and God, Son of Man and of God" (*ad Quirinum testimonia*, lib. 2, cap. 9).

HILARY OF POITIERS, FRANCE (c. 315-c. 367)

Hilary received a full education in philosophy and classics, becoming a Christian after marriage through the influence of biblical readings. During his office as bishop of Poitiers (after c. 353) he became a western champion of orthodoxy in the struggle against Arianism.

Hilary affirmed that Mary was a virgin before and after Jesus' birth, but there is no certain text about during his birth (De Trin. lib 3, N. 19; *Comm. in Mattheum*, cap. 1, N. 3). His condemantion of those who do not hold this begins a pattern that will continue until the Lateran Council 649, which will define Mary's perpetual virginity before, during, and after birth and pronounce an anathema on anyone who does not hold this (Lateran Council, can. 3). At the same time, Hilary's statements demonstrate the existence of other

Christian teachers who thought differently. He calls those who state that Jesus had blood brothers to be "very wicked men" (*Comm. in Matt.*, cap 1, N 3-4).

AMBROSE OF MILAN (C.339-397)

The work of Ambrose of Milan (c. 339-397) represents a new direction regarding Mary. Ambrose has the beginnings of a real Mariology that turns from Christological considerations to the person of Mary herself. As a youth, Ambrose received a thorough Greek, Roman as well as Christian training. After about 9 years of civil service, including a governorship of a Roman province, he was elected bishop of Milan.

For Ambrose, Mary is the special patroness of the virgins. He writes to them, "Receive then, O consecrated virgins, the spiritual rain that falls from this cloud (Mary) which will temper the burning desires of the flesh" (On Virginity, 13).[82] However, he accompanies this with a depreciation of marriage and sex that will unfortunately become more and more prevalent when emphasizing Mary's virginity. He writes, "Through a man and woman, flesh was cast from paradise; through a virgin, flesh was united to God" (Epist. 63, N. 33). When a bishop, Bonasus of Naissus (Yugoslavia) and others, maintained that Mary had more than one child, Ambrose replied that this was a "sacrilege" (On Virginity, 5, 35). For Ambrose, the celibate bishop, Mary's perpetual virginity is a model for virgins to follow.

The bishop of Milan presents Mary to his audience as an example of every virtue. A very influential text is in his explanation of the angel's annunciation to Mary with the words, "Hail, full of grace" (Luke 1:28). For Ambrose, this signifies a fullness of grace that no human being has ever received (Exp. Evangelii sec. Lucam, lib. 3, N. 9). The words of Ambrose, and others similar through the centuries would

---

[82]Palmer, p. 27.

be used by defenders of the doctrine of Mary's sinlessness and of the Immaculate Conception (her exemption from original sin). Both of these would be taught at the Council of Trent (Session 5 in 1546; Session 6, in 1547).

Ambrose also uses the unusual title "Mother of God" to describe Mary. He is one of the first writers of the west to do so (*Exp. Ev. sec. Lucam*, lib. 2, N. 26). Further discussion of this title and its implications will be found in the eastern writers of this period, where it will be connected with Mary's role as an intercessor and mediatrix.

Bishop Zeno of Verona (died c. 372) was probably influenced by Ambrose. He wrote, "What a marvelous mystery! Mary conceived as an incorrupt virgin; as a virgin, she gave birth; she remained a virgin after childbirth" *Tractatus, lib* 2, *Tr.* 8, 2). Zeno, like Ambrose, also addresses virgins and presents Mary as their model of holiness. She was "holy in body and spirit" and thus she deserved to carry the Savior (*Tract. lib.* 1, *Tr.* 5, 3; *lib.* 2, *Tr.* 8, 2).

ST. JEROME (c. 345-419 or 420)

Jerome received his classical education at Rome, where he was baptized at 19, although born of Christian parents. He was very much influenced by monastic and ascetic ideals, becoming a very influenctial spiritual director of prominent women in Rome. He was well known for his learning which he applied to the translation (into Latin) and exegesis of the scriptures.

In such an important role, Jerome had unprecedented and lasting authority in the west. He wielded that authority with a heavy hand to become a great western champion of the perpetual virginity of Mary. A certain Helvidius had claimed that Mary had a double honor: that of a virgin before Jesus' birth and then of a mother of other children afterward. In a widely circulated response, Jerome condemned Helvidius in no uncertain terms. Jerome's ascetic and celibate views surface in his reply: Virginity is definitely superior to marriage; to suggest Mary became at any time a mother through sex is "an outrage to the Virgin," a "defilement of the sanctuary of the Holy Spirit." Because Helvidius quoted Tertullian in support, Jerome calls the latter, "not a man of the church."

In the ardor of his defense, Jerome goes further than the scriptures in making Joseph both a virgin and a guardian of Mary's virginity, rather than a husband: "You say Mary did not continue as a virgin; I claim still more that Joseph himself on account of Mary was a virgin, so that from a virgin wedlock, a virgin son was born." *(Adv. Helvidium,* N 19)[83] In the same document, he states that the gospel "brethren of the Lord" were relatives, not blood brothers and sisters, and that even Joseph remained perpetually a virgin.

ST. AUGUSTINE, BISHOP OF HIPPO (354-430)

Augustine was the child of a pagan father and Christian mother, who saw to it he was raised as a Christian. As a youth, he was a serious student but at the same time entered an illicit union with a woman who bore him a son. Through the influence of Ambrose, Augustine converted from his former way of living, became a priest and finally a bishop of Hippo, Africa, about the age of 35.

Augustine became the most authoritative voice in Western Christian theology until the Middle Ages and Thomas Aquinas. He affirms the triple virginity of Mary in the words: "virgo concepit ... virgo peperit ... permansit," a virgin conceived, a virgin gave birth, a virgin remained afterward, (*Serm.* 190, N. 2). He even writes that the church would be proved false if Mary did not remain a virgin even during childbirth (*Ench. ad Laurentium,* cap. 34).

In a reply to Pelagius who taught the essential goodness of human nature, Augustine states that all human beings "with the exception of the Holy Virgin Mary" have sinned (*De natura et gratia,* 36 [42]). Like Ambrose, Augustine appeals

---

[83]Palmer, p. 26.

to Gabriel's "Hail full of grace" as a sign of the fullness of divine grace in Mary (*Sermo* 291, on the birthday of John the Baptist). Augustine's statements on Mary's virginity and sinlessness would influence later official church declarations on Mary's perpetual virginity and Immaculate Conception.

By way of summary, in contrast to the second century, third and fourth century western writers become more mariological than christological, with increased attention on the mother rather than on the child. The affirmation of the triple virginity of Mary becomes stronger and stronger. More focus is placed on Mary's virtues, especially her faith, obedience and sinlessness as models to admire and imitate. Her virginity is given exaggerated emphasis as a value for its own sake and a model for virgins who adopt a "superior" way of life to that of "ordinary" married people. These latter views come from clerics and male celibates who are very much influenced by the monastic and ascetic ideal.

The West furnishes no early evidence of a separate cult of Mary. However, as part of baptismal creeds, and as bound to Christ in teaching his human reality, prayers and liturgy could not isolate Christ from her. Her name and image would be before the Christian at baptism, the liturgies and private prayer. Cult to Christ would implicitly include Mary also. However, the stage is being set (and perhaps already occurring at popular levels) of a separate cult: she is patroness of virgins—would they not look to her for help from heaven as well as look to her as a model? This in turn would influence their friends and families to promote a more widespread popular devotion. Apocryphal literature as well as Christian writers recognize her high place in heaven; it is only a small step further to look to her for blessings as an intercessor.

10

The Road to Ephesus and Mary's Triumph: 200-431, Part II

EASTERN WRITERS

During this period, Marian writings proliferate in the East, and could easily fill a large volume. We will limit ourselves to significant changes and trends. The most prominent writers of the third century were Clement of Alexandria and Origen.

Clement of Alexandria (c. 150-c. 215) was probably born at Athens. He received a full Greek philosophical education and became a teacher and then head of the catechetical school of Alexandria, where he had great influence. Origen (c. 185-c. 254) was probably born in Alexandria, Egypt, receiving a Christian education from his parents. He studied under Clement and later took his place as head of the Alexandrian catechetical school. There he devoted himself to study as well as a strict ascetic life. He became a well known author and teacher not only in Alexandria, but later in Palestine.

Neither of the above insisted that Mary had to be a virgin during actual childbrith. In fact, the East does not share the West's obsession with Mary's perpetual virginity. There is not as much writing about it, and there was a variety of opinions until the middle of the fourth century. At this time, the great surge in monastic life may have prompted increased emphasis on Mary's perpetual virginity. Yet even Basil the Great (c. 329-379), founder of so many monasteries, does not regard it as part of faith, nor did some of his fellow bishops. At the same time, he stated that "no lover of Christ would ever listen to the idea that the Mother of God ever ceased to be a virgin" (Homily in S. Christi Generatio, N. 5).[84] Around 374, St. Epiphanius considers it abhorrent that Mary ever had marital intercourse and has Joseph (over 80!) with other previous children when he espoused Mary. He labels as heretics those who think differently (Panarion, *haer* 78, nn. 5-24). Yet the catechesis of Cyril of Jerusalem, while mentioning the virginal conception, does not propose for converts a belief in Mary's perpetual virginity.

From the beginning of the third century we find continued interest in the Eve-Mary parallel and in Mary's personal virtues. Clement compares Mary to the church; each is a loving mother and a virgin (Paedagogus, lib 1, cap. 6). Origen claims that Mary continually progressed in virtue, meditating daily on the Scriptures (*Hom 6 in Lucam*). He compares Mary to Eve in three homilies on Luke (6, 7, 8).

During the fourth century, some important events profoundly affected Mary's place in Christianity. First was the conflict with Arianism leading to the Council of Nicaea, 325. Arius and his followers argued that Christ, in view of his humanity, was subordinate to the Father, but with the first place in all creation. In sharp reaction to this, the council, assembled by the Emperor Constantine declared Christ "consubstantial with the Father" (Nicene Creed)—a creed still recited in Christian churches. This definition tended to make Christ remote by his absorption into the Trinity. This would be in contrast to his role as unique human mediator and path to the Father. A void could thus be left between God and humanity without this human link. It was a void that Mary would be very qualified to step into as the closest

---

[84]Most of the references to the eastern Fathers that follow are taken from W.J. Burghardt, "Mary in Eastern Patristic Thought," in J.B. Carol, ed., *Mariology*, Vol. 2.

person to Christ, both on earth and in heaven. At the same time, since Mary's son was consubstantial wth God, the way was open to giving her the later controversial title, "Mother of God."

The second event, was the adoption of Christianity as the official state religion by Constantine. The Nicean creed became an official government statement as well. This creed affirmed that Jesus became incarnate through the Holy Spirit and the Virgin Mary. Thus the *Virgin Mary* was given official status in the Roman empire, meaning that more attention would be given to her as a person.

Thirdly, and connected, Christians could emerge from their hidden place in the empire; the ages of persecution were over. The martyr was no longer the hero. Instead it was the monk and ascetic who led a life of "perfection." Monasteries and religious communities sprang up all over the empire. The patroness of celibates and ascetics was Mary, Queen of Virgins—someone they could look to as a model and also for help in fulfilling their difficult vocation. The fourth factor was a mysterious surge in popular devotion to Mary. This was certainly influenced and encouraged by monasticism, but it seems to have come from the people themselves, not from Christian writers or leaders, as we shall soon point out.

An important and very influential figure to pave the way to Ephesus, was a Christian poet, Ephrem of Syria (c. 306-373). Born in Mesopotamia, Ephrem came to Syria about 363. He lived an ascetic life in a cave and became well known as a holy man. Though never a priest or public official, he was respected as a volunteer worker in famine relief. Ephrem composed and promoted popular songs for Christian worship. These had been rare before his time. His prayers, poems and songs about Mary had widespread popularity and influence.

Ephrem's songs included direct praise of Mary in words such as, "Awaken your chorus, my harp, in praise of Mary the Virgin" (Hymns on the Blessed Mary, 18). He very explicitly describes Mary as an intercessor with words such as, "I call upon you, Mediatrix of the world; I invoke your prompt attention in my necessities,"[85] He also calls her "dispensatrix of all gifts" and mediatrix of the whole world."[86] In Ephrem, we find the Eve/Mary parallel elevated to new heights. Mary has an essential role in salvation as the cause of life in contrast to Eve, the cause of death (Sermo de domino nostro, n. 3). She is identified with the woman in Gen. 3:15-16 who will win a victory over the serpent (*Explanatio evangelii De concordantis,* Cap. 10, n 13).

Ephrem also continued the trend of emphasizing the virtues and sinlessness of Mary; e.g., in the following song lyric addressed to Mary and Jesus, he writes "You and your mother alone are perfectly beautiful in every way. There is no spot in you, O Lord, nor any stain in your mother" (Nisibis hymn, 27)[87] Quite remarkable is our poet's description of Mary's entry into heaven, carried through the air on the wings of Christ. She receives a garment of glory that also covers all humanity.[88] This theme of Mary's glorious entry into heaven will continue to be given more attention over the centuries until celebrated by a feast of Mary's assumption and defined as official dogma by Pius XII in 1950.

However, it is a contemporary of Ephrem, St. Epiphanius who furnishes us the most extraordinary information about popular cult of Mary. Epiphanius was born about 310 in Palestine and joined a community of monks in Egypt. There he became completely absorbed in language and scripture studies. He finally became recognized as a great leader in the Eastern church. In 367, the people of Salamis in Cyprus elected him as their bishop. He was known not only for his learning, but for his practical charity. His concern for orthodoxy led him to compose (around 375) a book called the *Panarion* (medicine chest) against 80 heresies of his time.

Very interesting for us are his observations on a group he nicknames "The Collyrians," (meaning, little loaf). They are

[85]J.B. Carol, ed., Vol. 2, p. 444.
[86]Cf. Note 86.
[87]Palmer, p. 23.
[88]J.B. Carol, ed., Vol. 2, p. 141.

a group, mostly women, who worship Mary as queen of heaven, even offering sacrifice to her: he notes that they prepare an altar, place bread on it, offer it in the name of Mary, and finally share it together. They appear quite numerous, not only located in areas west and south of the Black Sea, but also spread as far as Arabia. Their communities have women priests who baptize and offer sacrifices. Epiphanius condemns them, saying that only Father, Son and Holy Spirit should be adored, not Mary. Mary should not be a goddess, or be offered sacrifice, nor should women be appointed priests after so many generations of male leaders (Panarion, *haer.* 79).

The Collyrians are definitely a radical group about which we have no other information. But even the scant information in Epiphanius can lead us to educated guesses about them: if the radical group was so prominent, it would seem likely that there also existed widespread popular devotion and prayer to Mary that did not go that far. It would also appear that this "feminist" group is challenging male leadership in the church by assuming priesthood roles. In this challenge, they find Mary as an ideal role model as well as a source of divine blessings.

Strict a traditionalist as Epiphanius is, he never condemns prayers or cult of Mary: it is only the extremes of adoration that bother him. He even goes to remarkable lengths in his descriptions of Mary and her role. He expands the Eve typology by describing Mary as a "mother of the living" because she has brought life to the world (Panarion, *haer.* 78, n. 18). He even gives Mary the remarkable title *"Theotokos,"* meaning God-bearer or Mother of God.[89] This title had been appearing with increased frequency since the period of the Council of Nicaea. Around 319, Alexander of Alexandria used it in his condemnation of Arius. With Christ consubstantial with the Father, Mary is not just *Christophorus*, a Christ-bearer, but a *Theotokos*. Athanasius

---

[89]Cf. J.B. Carol, Vol. 2, p. 120 for references to sources of these *Theotokos* titles that follow.

likewise uses it several times. In his instructions for converts, Cyril of Jerusalem calls Mary the Virgin Mother of God. Basil the Great uses the expression as well as his younger brother Gregory of Nyssa. Gregory of Nazianzus even declares that anyone who does not say Mary is *Theotokos* is separated from the divinity. The three above men were friends of St. Ephrem and presented a united front against Arianism and Nestorianism in the East, where the use of this title initiated a great confrontation that would lead to Mary's triumph at Ephesus.

Epiphanius places unusual emphasis on Mary's holiness. He proclaims her as filled with every grace, holy, and worthy of honor, though not to be adored (Panarion, *haer.* 79, n. 7). If priests were permitted in the O.T., she would be a N.T. priest because she was worthy to receive God's son in her womb (Panarion, *haer.* 79, n. 3). Mary's "death" is equally holy and mysterious. Epiphanius writes that no one knows whether or where she died. He states that John did not take Mary to Roman Asia with him (lest male Christians continue a custom of taking virgins under their protection). Epiphanius' remarks are mysterious; he quotes the Apocalypse on the Woman clothed with the sun who is carried off by God to a hidden place to escape the dragon (Apoc. 12:13-14). However, he states that he really does not know whether she died or remains immortal (Panarion, 78, N. 11).

CONFLICTS AND TRIUMPH AT CONSTANTINOPLE AND EPHESUS

Despite the Council of Nicaea (325), Arianism persisted in many parts of the Roman Empire, especially the east. Constantius and Valens, pro-Arian eastern emperiors, put strong restrictions on Catholic worship in Constantinople until Valens' death in 378. The death of Valens gave the oppressed party a breath of hope, and they invited Gregory Nazianzus, friend of Ephrem, to the city as their special bishop.

While at Constantinople, Gregory preached a sermon[90] about a Christian virgin named Justine who called upon the Virgin when in danger of being forced to lose her virtue. Mary intervened miraculously and saved her. While Justine's story may be fictitious, it does illustrate that both preacher and audience believed in Mary's intercession and the possibility of her apparitions and miraculous interventions. This type of belief would grow through the centuries and culminate with the pilgrimages of millions of people to sites of Marian apparitions such as Lourdes and Fatima in the 20th century.

The hall or meeting place where Gregory addressed his people was called the Anastasia. An Arian mob tried to destroy it but it was saved. However, the tide changed in 380 when Theodosius, the new Eastern emperor became baptized as a Catholic and replaced the Arian bishop-Patriarch of Constantinople. After this, a church was built on the site of the Anastasia which became associated with healings and miracles attributed to the Virgin Mary.[91] It is significant that this place of triumph over Arianism is associated with Mary's name and presence. Perhaps this was already the case when Gregory gave his sermon about the power of Mary's intercession.

However, the final triumph of Mary would take place at Ephesus. The immediate preparatory stage was set at Constantinople, where in 428, a new patriarch, Nestorius, came into office. Nestorius and confreres from Antioch had become alarmed that the Arian reaction had so exalted Christ that he no longer seemed human. The Antiocheans tried to protect Christ's humanity by teaching that a complete divine person (the Logos, Son of God) from all eternity came on earth to dwell in a human body, which was fully a human person. This affected Mary: she could be called *Christokos* but not *Theotokos*.

Nestorius was only a short time in office when he presided

---

[90]From G. Ashe, p. 178.

[91]From G. Ashe, p. 180.

at a liturgy for a feast of Mary celebrated in his cathedral. A certain Proclus, later to become Patriarch, preached a sermon with superlative praises of Mary calling her among other things the bridal chamber of the Lord, the espousal place of the Word and human flesh, as well as the only bridge between God and Man.[92] At a climactic point in his sermon he called Mary, "the Holy *Theotokos* Mary." At this point, Nestorius arose from his episcopal throne, took the pulpit and declared that Mary was indeed worthy of all praises, but could not be called *Theotokos* because she could not mother the eternal Word, but only the Christ who began in her womb.

The news quickly spread that Nestorius had denied Mary was *Theotokos*. Cyril, Patriarch of Alexandria, a rival of Nestorius and Constantinople heard of the event. He quickly wrote up his case for Mary as Mother of God and sent it to Pope Celestine. The pope condemned Nestorius and sent the message to Constantinople by way of Cyril. However, Emperor Theodosius, along with Valentinian intervened and called a general council of the church at Ephesus where Nestorius could answer the charges. However Cyril and his allies prevented Nestorius' supporters from attending as well as the papal envoys. Then he illegally assumed leadership over the Council. Nestorius was put out of office and excommunicated. The deposition was confirmed by the emperor. Popular support rallied around Cyril. At Ephesus during the Council, crowds went through the streets chanting praises to Mary as Theotokos. It was like centuries before when the Ephesian people shouted, "Great is Artemis of the Ephesians" (Acts 19:34). Mary's triumph was complete.

At Ephesus, some months later, Cyril opened up a new era of Mary with a famous sermon given in the basilica of the *Theotokos* on Jan. 6, 432. He saluted Mary with the words, "Hail Mary, Mother of God (Theotokos)" a phrase that would be taken up for centuries by countless millions of Christians. In the sermon, he praised Mary as "the jewel of

---

[92]Palmer, p. 53.

the whole earth, the crown of virginity, the sceptre of orthodoxy, the indestructible temple, the unquenchable lamp" and many other superlatives. She is the one who has conquered the devil, freed creation from idolatry, brought baptism to believers, nations to repentance, and in whose honor churches are constructed all over the world.[93] Cyril did state that Christ had shone through her and was thus the real author of salvation. However, this was lost in the emotion charged praises of Mary with which his audience identified. Perhaps without realizing it, Cyril started a trend that would influence the whole Christian world.

With Nestorius fallen, Proclus, the great advocate of Mary, became Patriarch of Constantinople. Churches and shrines dedicated to Mary began to proliferate all over the Christian world. It is especially remarkable that many such churches were built over holy places of fertility goddesses. Santa Maria Maggiore in Rome took the place of a temple of Cybele, the great nature mother of Asia Minor. Another church in Rome was called "Santa Maria sopra Minerva," i.e., holy Mary built on top of Minerva. Geoffrey Ashe[94] points out that shrines of Aphrodite in Cyprus turned into shrines of Mary, where she is still honored by the title *Panaghia Aphroditessa*, (the holiness or sanctuary of Aphrodite). He notes that the goddesses transferred their functions to her: she guarded Rome like Cybele, mother of the gods; she watched over sailors like Isis as "Star of the Sea;" she cared for pregnant women like Juno; the title of "Queen of Heaven" was passed on to her from Isis, mother of Astarte. This process continued on to the early middle ages in Europe, where many of the prominent Marian cathedrals were erected over holy places of the great mother goddesses.

[93] Palmer, p. 50.
[94] p. 192.

THE CULT OF MARY IN THE EAST—200-432

When Cyril of Alexandria gave his famous sermon at Ephesus in 432, it took place in a "church of Mary, Mother of God." Cyril stated that churches in her honor "are erected all over the world."[95] Although Cyril does tend to exaggerate, this would seem to indicate a widespread cult of Mary at this time. In Constantinople, a few years before, Proclus spoke before Nestorius noting that it was a feast of the Virgin.[96] We saw that Gregory of Nazianzus preached in the Anastasia in Constantinople around 379, telling a story about Mary's response to prayer. The Anastasia was probably connected with some miracles or favors granted by Mary, since a church was built over the spot and the historian Sozomen[97] wrote later about Mary's power being manifested there.

The fact that Epiphanius noted (around 375) the widespread worship of Mary by the Collyrians shows that it had been around a considerable amount of time. Ephrem's writings in the same period indicated the existence of popular Marian cult. As early as ca. 319[98] we find the exalted title *Theotokos*, which was probably associated with cult of an earlier period, just as it was later. The title became so widely known that Julian the Apostate (331-363)[99] is reported to have said, "You never stop calling Mary Theotokos."

In the 1930's, a papyrus fragment was found of an ancient prayer addressed to Mary under the title *Theotoke*.[100] The Greek words are the same as a later widespread Latin invocation to Mary: *Sub tuum praesidium confugimus, Sancta Dei Genetrix* (We fly to thy patronage, Holy Mother

---

[95]Palmer, p. 50.

[96]Palmer, p. 53, in the use of the words, "the Holy Mary has called us together."

[97]From Ashe, p. 179.

[98]In Alexander of Antioch, announcing the defeat of Arius (Epist. Ad Alexandrum Constant. N. 12).

[99]Quoted by Cyril of Alexandria (Contra Iulianum, lib. 8).

[100]Cf. Carol, J., ed. Vol. 2, p. 121 for details.

of God). The date of the fragment, however, is disputed and estimated between the third and fourth centuries.

As we have noted in regard to the west, the joint association of Mary and Christ in worship goes much further back than the above dates. This is evidenced by her mention in early creedal formulas along with her son.

11

How Essential is Mary to Christianity?

In the Introduction, we pointed out the effects of the Protestant Reformation and the Vatican II Council. The place of Mary in Christian cult has been definitely on the decline. Is this for the better or for the worse? The answer to this question depends on how essential Mary is to Christianity. This in turn is only known through investigation of her biblical roots and then seeing at least how the first four centuries grew on these roots or departed from them.

THE N.T. ROOTS OF MARY'S ROLE IN CHRISTIANITY

Here we will try to draw some conclusions from our first seven chapters. We have seen that the early death/resurrection-centered preaching of Paul had an esteemed place for Mary as Mother of Jesus and as an early believer, but not as Mother of Christ. This was because the role of Christ was connected with Jesus' resurrection when God anointed him as Christ/Messiah by the Holy Spirit.

The gospel of Mark moved a step further by pushing back Jesus' messianic designation to his baptism. However this was a secret known to his disciples only through his death and resurrection. Mary and the family do not understand this secret and seem even to oppose him at least for a time. With Matthew, there is a decided deepening of the mystery. Jesus from the time of his birth is Messiah and son of God; his miraculous virginal conception is a sign of this. Thus Mary is now clearly portrayed as mother of the Messiah through an extraordinary divine action in a virginal womb. Matthew understands this as the culmination of a great divine plan working through history. The image of mother/ child is a permanent sign of God's scriptural plan of salvation. At the same time, the virginal birth guarantees Jesus' humanness as well as his divine origins. Thus Matthew plays an important part in establishing the inseparability of mother and son in Christian faith and teaching.

Luke goes even further by presenting a personal story of Mary that Christians can identify with. Like Sarah the great Mother of the Jewish people, Mary becomes a model and mother of believers. This mother role is a very active one as the carrier of blessings to her children. These children, imitating the Holy Spirit, respond with blessings and praise for their mother. In addition, Luke must respond to gnostic-influenced problems about the reality of Jesus' humanity, resurrection and continued presence, especially in the Eucharist. Mary becomes a key witness of Jesus' utter humanity in his birth and death. She also is a remembering mother and witness of the essential continuity and succession in Jesus' presence through the Spirit in the church. She is also a model of the believer who understands and appreciates the "impossible" divine scriptural plan to bring salvation to the world through the shame and weakness of the cross. In Jesus' public ministry Luke presents a new image of Mary as a mother and believer, rather than the apparently hostile picture in Mark.

John continues along the same lines as Luke. Within the suggested structure of the gospel's seven signs, Mary has a key role at the first and seventh interlinking signs. She is a remembering mother and essential witness of continuity and succession for the Christian community in establishing the reality and effects of Jesus' death. The seventh and first signs in turn link with the fourth sign of the loaves, thus establishing a eucharistic connection. The Apocalypse has the image of a cosmic mother in a conflict situation with the devil and the powers of evil. Mary has a part in this great mother image, but does not encompass it.

Thus the New Testament roots establish Mary as essentially related both to Christians and Christian teachings. Our next step will be to summarize what the first four centuries did to add or detract from this N.T. picture of Mary.

THE FIRST FOUR CENTURIES SEQUEL
TO THE NEW TESTAMENT

A thematic discussion will be more helpful than only a chronological one. In the early half of this period, Mary has a prominent place in resolving Christological problems. These concerned strong gnostic and docetic influences as well as Jewish questions about Jesus' origins. To answer these, Mary and the Virgin birth became a first line of defense to guarantee the human quality of Jesus' birth and death, as well as Jesus' real presence in the Eucharist. This meant that Mary and her virginal conception gradually took a central place in Christian beliefs along with the principal mysteries of the death and resurrection of Jesus. This meant that Mary's name and image was along side that of Christ during worship and liturgy. Without Mary, Christianity could have become gradually lost within the gnostic systems and mazes.

A second key area of Christological debate was the conflict with Arianism. Once more, emphasis on the Virgin birth helped to guarantee Christ's divinity in face of efforts to subordinate him to the Father. However, extreme reactions to Arianism had the effect of making Christ inaccessible and remote as part of the Trinity more than as the necessary human mediator between God and humanity. Christianity was almost left with a void. Consequently, Mary "stepped in" to fill this place in Christian practice and devotion, although Christ was still the "official" mediator. Without Mary, Christianity may have become more and more remote to the ordinary person and have fought a losing battle with other religious cults in the Roman empire.

The second important theme is that of popular devotion and personal interest in Mary herself. Even in the second century, the widespread interest in the *Protoevangelium of James* indicated popular interest in details about Mary's life and virtues. This interest continued in later infancy gospels and stories. Early church writers took interest in the Eve/Mary parallels and began to develop a theology about Mary and her role in salvation history. As time went on, this continuing process resulted in attributing primal and causal roles to Mary in the Christian economy of belief. Descriptions of her humility, obedience and motherhood role for Christians developed from this parallel.

St. Ephrem and St. Epiphanius, in particular, are witnesses to popular widespread cult of Mary in the middle fourth century. This appears to have been around for many decades. The Collyrian cult of Mary as goddess with corresponding sacrifices and a woman's priesthood was widespread and perhaps a revolt against a male dominated Christianity. Finally, the title of *Theotokos*, God-bearer, or Mother of God took a popular hold. It became a rallying point against Arianism and Nestorianism that led to Mary's triumph at the Council of Ephesus.

What we have described so far (with exception of Collyrianism) do not seem to be aberrations or deviations from the New Testament. First of all, the continued role of Mary was essential to preserve Christianity in the conflict for survival against gnosticism, Arianism and other challenges. Secondly, the development of a theology about Mary was part of the normal process of continual investigation and reasoned explanation of the scriptures and their implications.

However, quite different conclusions must be made regarding a third area: the monastic and ascetic influence on Mary's portrait. We have seen their laudable concern to present Mary as a patroness and example for virgins and celibates. However, the predominant tendency was to present virginity, modeled on Mary, as a superior state to marriage— a position without biblical support. In addition they declared (for the most part) that Mary was a perpetual virgin, not only before Jesus' birth, but even during and after his birth in order to strengthen the model for a life-long virgin or celibate. Thus their obsession with virginity led them to a position not supportable by the New Testament (except for before Jesus' birth). Even Mary's role as a wife to Joseph (found in the Scriptures) was either omitted or reduced to that of being a guardian of Mary's virginity. All of this, of course, had no connection with central Christian teaching until it was proclaimed as such by the Lateran Council in 649. The net result was that Mary could be imagined as a virgin and a mother but not really as a woman or wife— which indeed she was in the gospels.

Likewise, the excessive emphasis on Mary's sinlessness by this same group tended to create a less than human, almost "plastic" image of Mary. No doubt this was well-intentioned, in desiring to make her more and more like Christ (whose "sinlessness" has been misunderstood).[101] However, it was the beginning of a tendency to multiply Mary's privileges and set her far apart from the rest of the human race. Thus it became a far cry from the selfless, humble young woman in Luke who drew attention not to herself but God's work in her: "he who is mighty has done great things for me" (Luke 2:49).

Luke may be even warning against such a tendency in telling the story of the woman in the crowd who openly blessed Jesus' mother for the privilege of bearing him. Instead, Jesus replied that the blessing should rather be for those who hear God's word and keep it (Luke 11:27-28). Thus the monastic, ascetic influence in these centuries did well in their attention to Mary as a patroness and model.

---

[101]Cf. the study on this matter by V.P. Branick, "The Sinful Flesh of the Son of God (Rom. 8:3) A Key Image of Pauline Theology," *Catholic Biblical Quarterly* 47 (1985) 246-62.

Their example also helped to promote popular Marian cult. However, their excessive concern for her virginity made them part from the N.T.; it reduced Mary's image as a mother and served to depreciate the holy vocation of marriage. Fortunately, this did not destroy popular images of Mary. She was revered as a loving, personal mother with all the womanly qualities that accompanied that image. This went on despite the clouded image of Mary often presented by monks and celibates.

12

Mary in Early Christian Community

A Woman's Response
by
Carolyn Grassi

A major revolution of the twentieth century is the women's movement, which continues the push for equality in work, economics, politics, religion. Women are entering new careers in medicine, law, engineering, politics, management, aeronautics, religion and so on. At the same time, both men and women are facing the stress of job mobility, a societal emphasis on prestige and material success as measuring self-worth. America's high divorce rate affects women profoundly, as they usually end up heading households with less money and less emotional support than previous generations. With women's life-expectancy greater than men's, many women are spending their last years isolated, separated from their children and grandchildren who move to other parts of the country. Frequently elderly women live in severe poverty.

Women's social situation reflects her religious position as well. It is true that for centuries women have been excluded from positions of authority and leadership within the Church. While the priesthood remains outside woman's reach, new opportunities exist within theology, scripture and liturgical life for woman. Writers in both religion and psychology have shown over the last decade an increased concern for the feminine in religion. Jungian psychologists have uncovered the Greek goddesses as models for modern women's maturity and integration. Eric Neuman in his book *The Great Mother* explores the Virgin Mary as the central figure for woman's maturity, wisdom, creativity and compassion. Neuman says she appears repeatedly in history and culture as a "balance" to maleness. She is portrayed through art and ritual as wise, sensual, powerful. Her virginity is not a rejection of sexuality, but symbolizes her creative independence.

Henry Adams' magnificent prose in *Mont Saint Michel and Chartres* presents the Virgin of Chartres as a Goddess, Empress, Queen Mother. How remarkable that Adams began his study of the Virgin as a non-believer and was gradually won over by her presence at Chartres. He was open to her touching his psyche, experiencing, if you will, a melt down, a shift from a scientific study of the cathedral to an emotional and spiritual experience.

Notable women today like Rosemary Reuther, Christine Downing, Jean Bolen, Mary Daly insist on woman's equality in religious matters. Their writings have transformed the Trinity to include the femine principle. The God of the Old and New Testament, rises fresh as Mother, mid-wife, sister, daughter, spouse. Yet Mary needs inclusion intimately within the re-shaping of theological and scriptural studies. Debates continue over the "feminization" of the Trinity, with pros and cons on both sides. The emphasis in this chapter is the Virgin's presence throughout European church history via the arts. Before turning to that realm, let us look briefly at her pivotal place in the scriptures.

Mary came into her own at Pentecost, when the Holy Spirit visited her and the Apostles. She is first among women, as Christ is first among men. She bore in her womb God Incarnate. When we "see" the Spirit descend from heaven as in a Fra Angelico painting of the Annunciation, it is easy to imagine the Dove entering her and fusing as one. A marriage with the Paraclete, is a relationship of equality and respect. We know she had the major responsibility for forming the infant and child Christ. At the end of his life, in dying, Christ was concerned that his mother find support.

He asked his beloved friend John to care for her. Elsewhere in this book her place in Scripture has been emphasized.

It isn't surprising that the churches and cathedrals over hundreds of years singled out the Virgin. We see her in paintings, sculpture, cathedrals, shrines, cities as the woman who looms large on the Christian landscape. She is celebrated as Madonna, Queen, Virgin, Mother, Empress. In magnificent cathedrals as at Chartres her name is honored for over seven hundred years. In stone, in delicate detail, she stands with candles highlighting her lines of compassion, blackening her face in wisdom.

Is there any other woman who has inspired as many artists for as long a period of history? How is it possible her position in the American Catholic church has been nearly effaced? Even in the European churches, where she is celebrated, theologians have kept her on the outskirts. She remains in the realm of devotion. She is tolerated in piety, as a woman's phenomena. While Marian Theology was popular in the 1950's, she is again generally ignored by theologians.

Her popularity over the centuries has been a "grass roots" movement of the people. Artists made her rise as a great figure, sometimes equaling God the Father or overshadowing her son in cathedrals as at Chartres or Notre Dame de Reims, Paris and so on. Theologians like Thomas Aquinas in the Middle Ages built enormous written monuments to the Trinity. Their words rivaled the architecture that housed the Virgin. She was theologized into non-importance, culminating in the Second Vatican Council's pushing her to the periphery of Church life. In the later 20th century she continues among those women who exist on the boundaries of religion, understanding the mark suffered for centuries by the outcasts, whether labeled as "non-kosher," witches, fortune tellers, sorceresses, sphinxes, goddesses.

Modern dismissals of Mary seem to have dealt her a death blow in the American Catholic church. The Second Vatican Council in building bridges to non-Catholic denominations, apologized for Marian devotion and minimized her place in theology. Americans, more literal than the Europeans, followed the details of the Vatican Council—doing away with many rituals connected with the Virgin. The Catholic Church in the Latin countries was too steeped in history to take the Council up on every point. They experienced the comings and goings of papal decrees and councils. These churches would modernize, but also preserve what was beautiful and rich from the past. Their devotion to the Virgin was ancient and rooted in artistic and cultural life.

So, it was impossible to erase a presence that has existed for years in the life of a people. The Virgin stood for the feminine in a people's pysche or soul. If she were to go entirely, then a masculine culture would dominate. Certainly France would no longer be herself, nor would Italy. This close identity between the Virgin and the feminine principle is touched on by the French sculptor Auguste Rodin. In the cathedrals of France he perceived a womanly shape and uniqueness. He wrote this:

> The benedictions of the city and of the world are its women. Bearers of life, sensitive forms of hope and joy, substance of all masterpieces, so close to Nature they are! Woman is the true Holy Grail and she is never more beautiful than kneeling; the Gothics thought of this. A church from the outside is shaped like a woman....

With an artistic sensitivity he saw Her in every woman and particularly in the cathedrals. He expressed it this way:

> Is there not everywhere here (in the cathedrals) a magnificent eulogy to woman formulated in the plastic language of stone? And if the Virgin is first to be honored by it, is it not she who opens to us the gates of springtime? Do we not discover the Universe thanks to her?

Even before the first World War, Rodin mourned for modern society's insensitivity to the great and tender art of Nature, the cathedrals, women and the Virgin. He praised the female element as strong, eternal, irreplaceable. Rodin saw the Virgin as complement and spouse of God. He opened his eyes and saw the feminine presence everywhere. It is possible for us to recover this insight.

We know men and women are traveling in our times to Greek temples and locations of the ancient goddesses. They are looking into Hellenic myths for personal meaning. They are uncovering stories, gazing into the faces of Greek goddesses, drawing on powerful female images. In her book *Goddesses Within* Jean Bolen gives specific aids for women to foster certain goddess qualities. Bolen's is a "how to" approach for women maturing. Christine Downing in her book *The Goddess* was the first to suggest specific female Greek models as helpful for maturity or what Jung named "individuation."

Maybe the American genius for the practical, our engineering know-how, makes us look at antiquity for direct clues to personal growth. Yet why ignore what Christianity offers in the powerful and human figure of the Virgin. The dominant tone in American religious culture is and has been Calvinism or Puritanism, which has little use for the Virgin Mary. Yet, American Catholicism sprung from immigrant European churches, whose roots lead back to an inexhaustible art and history of the Virgin. The essence of Catholicism has always included a strong presence of Mary. As modern men and women find in the ancient gods and goddesses meaningful metaphors for their lives, we need not apologize for the European emphasis in history and art on the Virgin equaling the Greek deities.

The search for Christ occurs in study of Scripture, Church history and theology. Through debate and writings, doctrines competed, heresies were suppressed by papal decrees and Councils. As said earlier, the Virgin's history is found outside official pronouncements. She exists in the customs of countries like France, Italy, Poland and Spain. She shines in the art of Fra Angelico, Leonardo da Vinci, Raphael, Botticelli and others. She reigns in the gorgeous cathedrals built in her honor like "Notre Dame" de Reims, Rouen, Chartres, Paris, Coutances. In Spain's Monserrat, in Poland's

Jasna Gora, in hundreds of Russian icons we see her strong, vivid, dark face, dear to a people's psyche.

In these ancient portrayals of the Virgin she endures for hundreds of years as vital, strong, independent, compassionate and human. The queens and powerful women of the Catholic countries along with ordinary people promoted her cause, insisting that her churches fit her position as Empress or Queen. They obtained the best materials and finest artists. Countless men and women worked freely to furnish her homes. The present-day candles lit before her statues all over Europe continue the old custom of decorating her residence with light and flowers. Who remains unmoved by Chartres Cathedral, when standing in her sanctuary before the world's most beautiful stained glass.

Finding the ancient Virgin as contemporary is a work of discovery and adventure. She exists, as she always has, patiently waiting for our return. Her place in painting, sculpture, architecture, custom complements Christ's place in our theology. She lives in the Catholic psyche, in its cultures, as Christ does in its dogma and formal liturgical life. This implies that a people's imaginative life is on a par with their intellectual life, that God acts not only through theologians and the official church, but through musicians, painters, scuptors, artisans, patrons, the people in general. Self-expression by an individual, a people, a country vies for equality alongside theologians and church officials. For as Hegel said, a people's feeling for God springs from their soul, temperament, habits, needs. When the feminine presence is submerged for too long, "She" surfaces or revives herself through ancient and modern images. So it is with the Virgin.

While Christ and the church are studied in texts, the Virgin is found in a different sort of way, on the tabloids of stained glass, in statues, paintings, in the legends of places like Provence where custom claims Mary sailed the Mediterranean and spent her last years in southern France. The entire countryside of Provence exudes an aura concerning early Christian women. The mountain of Sainte Baume, overlooking Aix-en-Provence, claims the cave where Mary Magdalen lived the last thirty years of her life. An ancient Roman sarcophagus is said to be her tomb in this cave, while in Avignon Saint Martha presides as patron of that territory. In the granite crypt of the Mediterranean church at Sainte Marie's beach the statue of the dark-skinned Saint Sarah is revered by countless gypsies.

Who can prove or disprove such legends. It is beside the point, these stories carry power. They evoke the feminine presence by their imaginings. They fill a void that the institutional church fails to do, namely to give a womanly portrayal of God. How striking that religion in Provence is strongly feminine, for this area is the birthplace of courtly love and Western poetry. Numerous artists such as Cezanne, Pissaro, Van Gogh, Picasso and others, made their home in southern France, feeling at home in its warm, earthy milieu. The great world religions began in this general area of the Mediterranean basin.

The present challenge is to uncover Mary's presence so richly pervading European culture. If we Americans admire ancient Greece for her gods, we need also the Catholic countries of Italy, France, Spain, Latin America, Poland, Portugal, Hungary and the Greek Orthodox countries to see how the Virgin appears in the psyche of these peoples. At the same time, our friends in psychology, who "use" or interiorize the ancient Greek goddesses in practical matters, show us how to "adapt" what we see, hear, read, learn of the Virgin into a personal experience. For example, they suggest women call on Diana to foster a spirit of adventure and daring, Demeter for closeness to earth, Venus for the flowering of love and sensuality.

So, too, Mary for almost two thousand years has built up a repertoire of roles. Just look at the variety of names she wears in her litany, or notice her position in renditions of the Annunciation; sometimes she is humble, other times assertive, vivacious. In the Visitation her position varies from one of student to Elizabeth to that of "mother of my Lord." Thus, in this latter role, Mary stands on the sanctuary screen at Notre Dame inclining her head to Elizabeth who bows to her brilliancy.

We see her as Empress ruler, wise woman on her throne at Chartres, or her sensuality startles us in certain Italian Madonnas as with her gorgeous form in the Leonardo painting at the Louvre "Saint Anne and the Virgin." So through the genius of various cultures and people she appears near us in human form, as she does at the side altars of every Catholic European church, like Saint Germaine des Pres in Paris, where after a stroll on the fashionable Left Bank boulevard one enters the ancient church and immediately sees the 13th statue of the Virgin of Compassion smiling over candles at the back door. Or an hour from Paris, in the town of Chartres she appears as the Queen Empress, the Seat of Wisdom, and we realize in her cathedral how great is her power. Yet, even here her might is tempered by tenderness and compassion, for the glory of Chartres is in its stained glass jewels set as roses, the ancient symbol of woman. In this church also legend claims the Virgin's chemise, or birthing garment, is preserved as a protecting relic for the people. Within the enormous, powerful boundaries of this cathedral with its magnificent towers and flying buttresses, a sheer, delicate garment testifies to the humanity of this female side of God. At Reims in the month of August the cathedral is decked out in magnificent tapestries, hundreds of years old, telling the story of the Virgin from her conception in Saint Anne to her Coronation as Queen of Heaven and Earth.

In the end, it isn't necessary to work up a so-called new conception of God to meet women's need for equality. In fact, such efforts at transforming God may only repeat what we have, a male God with a new name. Christ handed over the treasure of his heart, this beloved woman, to grace the world. How lovely and moving her presence appears in the faces of countless women who served as models for artists, who sprung up in cultures because they were already known and loved by the people. Maybe her living "outside" the boundaries of theology gave her a freedom to act on the sensibilities of her artists and ordinary people, so that, at times, she was both worshiped and intimately near.

Language both reflects and changes culture. The current American Church's push for a so-called "neutral language" is depersonalizing. We are not angels, we are humans, male and female. Granted that integration of both principals is valuable, but maturity dosn't mean arrival at a neutered state. Particularity, the uniqueness of the individual must be preserved in an age where life is cheapened, where human beings are dispensable and replaceable, without the blinking of an eye. Intimacy in love for the majority of people means a distinctive complement between a man and a woman. This is not inequality or a split. Sexuality is a free gift among equals. Why should our religion be "de-sexed," without any male or female connotations? Certainly if the arts as literature, ballet, the theater, opera, sculpture did away entirely with such uniqueness in quest of a neutral idiom, we'd be in a sorry state. The feminine has co-existed with the masculine in the Church, she has survived through visualizing and naming of the Virgin. Today it's time to recognize the power of this woman, archetype, persona, goddess. It seems ridiculous that the Church that originally celebrated her importance has lost sight of her, while modern psychologists admire her and stress her powerful place in history and culture.

The challenge today with woman's heightened awareness as an equal partner to man, means including woman in every aspect of religious expression. Literature reveals the beauty, mystery and potency of both the masculine and feminine. To exactly define these terms is not easy or even possible. But to dismiss them as passé, to try using a "de-sexed" language in liturgical and theological life comes close to making religion abstract, other-worldly and boring.

Today women and feminist men are thrilled at re-finding the Virgin as a powerful persona, as the feminine Spirit fleshed out in a woman's form. Certain rituals are offering her a central place. She is claiming her rightful position alongside the Father and Son as temple, house of the Spirit, as partner with God, as she invites all women to celebrate their equality and uniqueness with her; as she offers her hands of compassion, her words of wisdom to men and women.

In celebration of women and Mary's continued presence, I have written the poems that follow.

13

Celebrating Mary

Poems
by
Carolyn Grassi

1. *Annunciation*
2. *The Virgin's Death*
3. *Resurrection*
4. *Apocalypse*
5. *Queen of Heaven and Earth*
6. *Star of the Sea.*

Annunciation

she   the figure drawn   painted   year after year
a room for revelation   an angel messenger enters
a curtained space illumined by words
spinning stars touch the trembling earth
the response needed was yes   yes   without hesitation
a transparent blue—rose window light
great love adhered to her wish
she shaped his secret under her heart
giving her eyes' color   subtle hands   rhythmed cadences
her strong arms   thick dark hair   reflective brow
she drew a tiny perfect form from the ancient soul
    of the universe
she anticipated the child maturing in her center

The Virgin's Death

she closed her eyes
John and Peter searched for her pulse
she left without fanfare
featured in her descendants

the sculptor resurrected her sequence
as she stood in the doorway
urgency in her eyes
bearing the child full-term
she kneaded yeast in the dough
she drew the grape-vine's liquid
she gave him the lily of the valley's aroma
she pointed to the sparrows creating their nests
she offered a cup of water to a stranger with grace

she encouraged his dreams
saying he was welcome whenever...
without control   no strings attached
she lived as before   intently silent
waiting for God's nuances to surprise her

the sculptured effect on the cathedrals
captures her contemplation
having closed her eyes
her lips form the pleasure
as Light grows emphatic

afterwards her reunion at the double thrones
she inclines her head as Christ offers the crown

Resurrection

God's son in childhood pleasured your home
he tried touch the white furred dove
he drank honey　sheltered his eyes at noon under olive
groves
he laughed at the cicadas in the summer night
he pointed to the caravans approaching in moonlight

at the finale his white clothes creased in four on the cave's
shelf
you folded your handkerchief over your heart　there was no
recompense
only keeping sentinel as years earlier when the daffodils
trembled
when the sea-breeze penetrated the August desert
when the planets drew close in alignment
for the Morning Star rising in the east

Apocalypse

if you wish me   I'm underground
in the labyrinth   in the crypt
a pink lotus in dark waters

I tower over September wheat fields
twin towers set on a city's slope
a welcoming position held for centuries

you arrive home through my portal
my table weighed with wine   fruit   bread   milk
my alcoves ablaze with candles   my roses caressing the light

my hands vessel healing   I listen with care
I believe in your resurrection
I shape your names with bronze and turquoise

Anne   Elizabeth   Judith   Rebecca   Sarah
the snake and crescent moon under your feet
the twelve stars circling your head

Queen Of Heaven And Earth

she is clothed in a blue dress before a red background
her throne an ordinary chair   she nourishes the divine child

the sun makes rendezvous in her bronze tower
her windows welcome every season into the rose

her presence is fluid in the sanctuary screen
leaves of the palm plant spread open in prayer

the great dove pierces the arc in late March
he escorts the tongues of summer fire

thus the argent core and lily please her
God's strength is folded in her arms

her cathedral is situated in the city
her towers visible in the country

Star Of The Sea

Regina Maris   on the horizon of the east

my ship follows your assumption
a light hovering in darkness

you persist among the elm leaves
lustering their midnight surfaces

you tune the navigational instruments
you hold rudder and tacks in your concern

you channel the roaming distractions
into a creative enterprise

your singular purpose delights
you accompany the fishing vessels out and in

yours the clemency after doubtful nights
yours the glow spotted at the beginning

you promise rendezvous in the west

Books and Articles Consulted

Alfaro, J. "The Mariology of the Fourth Gospel: Mary and the Struggle for Liberation," *Biblical Theology Bulletin* 10 (1980) 3-16.

Adams, Henry, *Mont Saint Michel & Chartres* (Marietta, Ga.: Larlin, 1978).

Ashe, Geoffrey, *The Virgin* (London: Routledge & Kegan Paul, 1976).

Audet, J.P., "L'annonce à Marie," *Revue Biblique* 63 (1956) 364-74.

Bolen, Jean, *Goddesses in Every Woman: A New Psychology of Women* (N.Y.: Harpers, 1984).

Brown, Raymond E., *The Birth of the Messiah*, (Garden City, N.Y.: 1977)

Brown, R.E., *The Community of the Beloved Disciple* (N.Y.: Paulist, 1979).

Brown, R.E., *The Gospel According to John (i-xii),* (Garden City, N.J.: Doubleday, 1966).

Brown, R.E., *The Gospel According to John (xiii-xxi),* (Garden City, NJ.: Doubleday, 1970).

Brown, R.E., Donfried, K.P., Fitzmyer, J.A., Reuman, J., *Mary in the New Testament* (Phila., Pa.: Fortress, 1978).

Buby, Bertrand, *Mary the Faithful Disciple*, (Mahwah, N.Y.: Paulist, 1985).

Carol, Eamon R., (Junniper B) *Mariology*, 2 vols. (Milwaukee: Bruce 1954, 55).

Carol, E.R., *Understanding the Mother of Jesus* (Wilmington, Del.: M. Glazier, 1974).

Cole, Eugene, "What Did Luke Mean by *Kecharitōmenē?*" *American Ecclesiastical Review* 139 (1958) 228-239.

Collins, Adela, *The Apocalypse* (Wilmington, Del.; M. Glazier, 1979).

De Goedt, M., "Un Scheme de Révélation dans le Quatrième Evangile," *New Testament Studies* 8 (1962) 142-150.

Downing, Christine, *The Goddess: Mythological Images of the Feminine* (Crossroad, 1984).

Ellis, P. *The Genius of John, A Composition—Critical Commentary on the Fourth Gospel* (Collegeville, Minn.: Liturgical Press, 1984).

The Fathers of the Church, The Apostolic Fathers, trans. G.G. Walsh (N.Y.: Christian Heritage Inc., 1947).

The Fathers of the Church, St. Justin Martyr, trans. T.B. Falls (N.Y.: Christian Heritage Inc., 1948).

Fiorenza, E., "Composition and Structure of the Book of Revelation," *Catholic Biblical Quarterly* 39 (1977) 344-366, esp. 353-366.

Fitzmyer, J., *The Genesis Apocryphon of Qumran Cave 1* (Rome: Biblical Institute Press, 1971 revised ed.).

Giblin, C.H., "Reflections on the Sign of the Manger," *Catholic Biblica Quarterly* 29 (1967) 87-101.

Giblin, C.H., "Suggestion, Negative Response and Positive Action in St. John's Portrayal of Jesus," *New Testament Studies* 26 (1980) 197-211.

Girard, M. "La Composition Structurelle Des Septs Signes dans le Quatrième Evangile," *Sciences Religieuses* 9 (1980) 315-324.

Grassi, Joseph, *The Secret of Paul the Apostle* (Maryknoll, N.Y.: Orbis, 1978).

Grassi, Joseph, *God Makes Me Laugh: A New Approach to Luke* (Wilmington, Del.: Michael Glazier, 1985).

Grassi, J., "The role of Jesus' Mother" in John's Gospel: A Re-appraisal," *Catholic Biblical Quarterly* 48 (1986) 67-80.

Harrington, W.H., *Mark* (Wilmington, Del.: M. Glazier, 1979).

Hennecke, Edgar, W. Schnecmelcher, ed., R. Mc L. Wilson, 2 Vols., English Trans. *New Testament Apocrypha* (Philadelphia: Westminister, 1963, 1965).

Karris, Robert, *What Are They Saying About Luke-Acts?* (Mahwah, N.Y., Paulist, 1979).

Laurentin, R., *Structure et Theologie de Luc I-II*, (Paris: Gabalda, 1957).

LaVerdiere, E., *Luke*, (Wilmington, Del.: M. Glazier, 1980).

McHugh, J., *The Mother of Jesus in the New Testament* (Garden City, N.Y.: Doubleday, 1975).

Meier. John, *Matthew*, (Wilmington, Del.: M. Glazier, 1981).

Minear, P.S., "The Beloved Disciple in the Gospel of John. Some Clues and Conjectures," *Novum Testamentum* 19 (1977) 105-123.

Neumann, Erich, Manheim, R., trans. *The Great Mother: An Analysis of the Archetype* (Princeton, N.J.: Princeton Univ., 1964).

Osiek, Carolyn, *Galatians*, (Wilmington, Del.: M. Glazier, 1980).

O'Toole, R.F., *The Unity of Luke's Theology: An Analysis of Luke-Acts* (Wilmington, Del.: M. Glazier, 1984).

Pagels, Elaine, *The Gnostic Gospels* (N.Y.: Random, 1979).

Palmer, Paul F., *Mary in the Documents of the Church* (Westminster, Md.: Newman, 1952).

Robinson, James, gen. ed., *The Nag Hammadi Library* (N.Y.: Harper, 1981).

Rodin, Auguste, Geissbuhler, E., trans. *Cathedrals of France* (Redding Ridge, CT.: Black Swan, 1981).

Stanley, David, *Christ's Resurrection in Pauline Soteriology* (Rome: Pont. Bibl. Inst., 1961).

Serra, A.M., Trans. B. Mollat, *Marie à Cana, Marie Pres de La Croix* (Paris: Editions du Cerf, 1983).

Tambasco, A.T., *What Are They Saying about Mary* (Ramsey, N.J.: Paulist, 1984).

Vawter, B., "The Gospel According to John," in *The Jerome Biblical Commentary* (Englewood Cliffs, N.J.: Prentice-Hall, 1968).

Index

Scripture Index

OLD TESTAMENT

NEW TESTAMENT